GOYA

WORK, LIFE, DREAMS…

GOYA

WORK, LIFE, DREAMS...

JOSE MANUEL PITA ANDRADE

Sílex

© Silex® 1989
I.S.B.N.: 84-7737-006-0
Layout: Juan Manuel Domínguez
Traslated by: Evelyne Colchero
Depósito Legal: M. 37.395-1989
Printed in Spain by

CONTENTS

To the memory of Francisco Javier Sánchez Cantón,
Enrique Lafuente Ferrari, José Camón Aznar,
Xavier de Salas Bosch, José Gudiol Ricart, Valentín de Sambricio
and Juan Antonio Gaya Nuño, all distinguished Goya scholars,
whom I am proud to call my friends and masters.

INTRODUCTION

A general stock-taking of the situation of Spanish painting after the so-called "Golden Age" (which can more or less be identified with the 17th century), will lead us to the conclusion that the arrival of a French Bourbon king on the Spanish throne following the death of Charles II in 1700 coincided with one of the greyest periods in Spanish art. The new king, Philip V, had to resort to artists from abroad, mainly French, because the creative vein in court circles seemed to have petered out after the great Baroque painters like Francisco Rizi, Carreño and Claudio Coello had disappeared. With a few exceptions, the first half of the century known as the "Age of Light" in Spain did not produce painters capable of carrying on the great heritage of the previous century. French artists in the first place and later Italians had to fill the gap, but at the same time this brought about a complete break with the artistic tradition that had existed in Madrid during the reigns of the last Hapsburg kings.

Goya's arrival on the scene in the midst of this artistic upheaval is one of the most surprising and unexpected events in the history of Spanish painting. Admittedly, in the same year that Goya was born (1746) decisive steps were being taken to create an Academy to promote the arts. The institution was finally established in 1752 under the name of Royal Academy of Noble Arts of San Fernando and its first efforts are not to be underestimated. However, all the measures taken to promote the education of young artists would probably have been of little avail if it had not been for a genius, in this case in the shape of an uncouth Aragonese, who opened up new horizons in the field of painting. Goya's personality, contradictory as it was, brought about far-reaching changes in the manner of understanding a painting, although in many respects he was not inconsistent with his time. With regard to Goya's many different and even contrasting styles, one of the best Spanish experts on this subject, Sánchez Cantón, wrote: "If some

9

absurd cataclysm were to wipe out the figure of Goya and leave nothing but his works, the only common feature that art critics could recognize in them would be their very Spanish flavour; their other characteristics would cause critics to attribute them to different and even unrelated artists, some not even contemporary ones"[1]. The changes in style to be found in Goya's works are the best heralds of what was to happen in 19th and 20th-century painting.

Goya lived long enough to be a witness to a number of events that ushered in a new age in modern history. He experienced the ideological crisis that led up to the French Revolution; he followed the tragic events ensuing from the storming of the Bastille; he observed at first hand the corrupt atmosphere of Charles IV's court and lived through the dramatic events of the Peninsular War. He experienced Ferdinand VII's despotic rule and finally, almost 80 years old, he chose to go into exile. His life, astride the 18th and 19th centuries, and his work are therefore particularly interesting for their symbolic character. His paintings, drawings and engravings reveal both the man and the artist, although the image of his time that he reflects in his works is a very personal and sometimes impassioned one. But this passion conveys an enthusiasm that seems youthful because it looks forward into the future. For this reason his works express such a store of human feeling.

They convey a state of emotional tension that makes the observer search for hidden meanings that shroud the figure of the artist in a veil of mystery. In the light of certain texts and documents Goya's life has been viewed with a great deal of imagination, especially under the impulse of the Romantic movement. No other artist's life has produced so many biographical novels, which in turn gave rise to a popular myth about Goya.

1. See Sánchez Cantón (1951), page 2; English edition (1964), page 10. First and foremost I would like to stress the importance of this work by Sánchez Cantón; it is one of the most serious studies that have been published about the great artist. As one of Francisco Javier Sánchez Cantón's closest collaborators in Madrid for many years, I was fortunate enough to witness some of his important discoveries concerning Goya. These few lines are intended as an acknowledgment and tribute to his memory.

GOYA IN THE EYES OF CRITICS AND HISTORIANS

In Goya's biography there is scope for the most exaggerated judgements. Some present him as a great patriot in the dramatic years of the Napoleonic invasion; others consider him *afrancesado* or "Frenchified", that is, an enthusiast of French ideas. Some point out his religious feelings, while others exalt him as a free-thinker. He has been called a "philosopher-painter", whereas, as a reaction against this opinion, others have stressed the evident vulgarity in the subject-matter of some of his etchings. His relations with the Duchess of Alba have given rise to all manner of fanciful conjectures. Completely contradictory attitudes have been adopted not only by the writers of "biographical" novels, but also by recognized art historians. This controversy is possible because, much as we know about the details of his actual life, there are nonetheless important aspects of his personality that escape us.

Until 1982 Goya's correspondence had only been published in extracts and, worse still, often omitting whole paragraphs if the biographer felt that these could alter the image that he had intended to present of the artist. This occurred, for example, with Francisco Zapater, who used Goya's correspondence with his uncle Martín[2] in a pamphlet published in 1868 to counter works written in France by Matheren and Yriarte in 1858 and 1867, which in turn were also biased. In a masterly study on *"La situación y la estela del arte de Goya"*, the critic Lafuente Ferrari correctly observed that these two French writers, "true pioneers in

---

2. Martín Zapater (? - 1802) was without doubt Goya's closest friend. A merchant resident in Saragossa, Zapater kept up correspondence with the artist at least from 1775 until 1801. This correspondence was published, although only in part, by his nephew Francisco and despite considerable omissions is extremely interesting. The *Cartas a Martín Zapater* (published under this title by Xavier de Salas and Mercedes Agueda, with an introduction and numerous notes) contain a wealth of invaluable facts to reconstruct Goya's "human profile" as offered in this book.

the bibliography on Goya, have been the scapegoats against whom all later Spanish biographers have directed their attacks in a controversy apparently aimed more at disclosing curious mistakes than at appreciating the worthwhile information that these writers contributed towards our knowledge of the artist, including invaluable memories that would otherwise have been lost for posterity"[3].

If art historians and biographers tended to indulge in such heated arguments, this was because Goya represented a transcendental change in the manner of understanding the work of an artist: his manner of expressing himself was based on non-artistic considerations and thus on the stand he took on the ideological issues of his time. Goya's early French biographers insisted on his importance as a critic of the society he lived in. Charles Yriarte converted him into "the incarnation of the revolutionary spirit... a sort of Spanish Rousseau; in a rather light-minded tone he begins his work by saying that he intends to show the part Goya played as a thinker in the ideological movement of his time"[4] (Lafuente Ferrari). This manner of interpreting the personality of a man who was first and foremost a

The first works to be written about Goya were published by Matheron (1858) and Yriarte (1867) in France. Both are very interesting, although at times they present the artist in a false light.

painter should not prevent us from admitting that there were also critics in France at an early stage who were interested in Goya as an artist and as a person. About 10 years after his death he is mentioned by Viardot, although rather misleadingly, in his work on Spanish painters[5]. During the following two decades other works with varying degrees of accuracy were published, among them enthusiastic appreciations by writers like Théophile Gautier or Baudelaire[6]. This great poet wrote: "Goya's chief merit lies in having created credible monsters. His monsters are

---

5. Louis Viardot wrote a number of works, published from 1835 on, about the Fine Arts, museums and principal artists in Spain, which include early references to Goya. See Bibliography.
6. Much could be written on the subject of Goya's influence on French writers and artists during the nineteenth century. There is abundant bibliographical material about the matter. See Lipschutz's important work (1972) with numerous quotations. With reference to Théophile Gautier, see pages 118-119.

---

3. See Lafuente Ferrari (1947), page 24.
4. See Lafuente Ferrari (1947), page 24.

GOYA

PAR CHARLES YRIARTE

SA BIOGRAPHIE

LES FRESQUES, LES TOILES, LES TAPISSERIES, LES EAUX-FORTES

ET

LE CATALOGUE DE L'ŒUVRE

AVEC CINQUANTE PLANCHES INÉDITES

D'APRÈS LES COPIES DE TABAR, BOCOURT ET CH. YRIARTE

PARIS

HENRI PLON, IMPRIMEUR-ÉDITEUR

RUE GARANCIÈRE, 10

1867

Tous droits réservés.

feasible and harmonious. Nobody has penetrated as far as Goya into the world of the possible absurd. All those distortions, those beast-like faces, those fiendish grimaces, are packed with humanity... The meeting-point between reality and fantasy is impossible to distinguish; even the most subtle critic is incapable of tracing the dividing-line, in such a way is Goya's art transcendental and life-like at the same time"[7].

If we turn to Spanish bibliography, we find that writers such as Valentín Carderera and Francisco Zapater contributed towards preserving Goya's image. But a year after the latter published his *"Noticias biográficas"*, a curious *"Calendario civil... con los santos mártires defensores de la Independencia y Libertad de España"* was edited in Madrid, in 1869, which listed "St. Francisco Goya y Lucientes, famous painter and great patriot... one of the most illustrious victims of Ferdinand VII's despotic rule". So our painter is

converted into a martyr for the freedom of his country, as has been revealed by Lafuente Ferrari[8].

Without going in detail into the numerous works on Goya published during the 19th century in France and Spain, we should mention some of the most important ones; these include studies by Cruzada Villaamil on the tapestries (1870), Lefort on the etchings (1877), Count de la Viñaza with important discoveries about Goya's life and works (1887) and also Araujo (1896), in spite of his rather narrow-minded view of the artist. The century closed with an important exhibition in the Ministry of

7. This text is quoted from the Spanish edition published by Espasa-Calpe (Baudelaire, Charles: *Pequeños poemas en prosa*, 1st edition, Buenos Aires, Col. Austral, 1948, page 142). This famous French critic wrote about Goya on various occasions, the first probably on October 15th 1857 in "Le Présent", Paris, in an article entitled *"Quelques caricaturistes étrangers: Goya"*. See also Guinard's article (1967) quoted in the Bibliography.

8. See Lafuente Ferrari (1947), page 330.

Charles Baudelaire (1821-1876) and Théophile Gautier (1811-1872) did much to popularize Goya in France during the age of Romanticism. The so-called "Goya legend" originated primarily north of the Pyrenees.

Public Education and Fine Arts in Madrid in 1900.

As far as the 20th century is concerned, it is difficult to offer a compendium of the many studies that have been published on Goya's life, works or partial aspects such as his drawings or etchings. Up till the first centenary of his death, in 1928, the chief works were those by Loga, Calvert, Beruete and Mayer, that deal mainly with Goya's paintings, whereas Pierre d'Achiardi, Delteil, Sánchez Rivero and others are concerned with his drawings and etchings. In 1924 the publisher Calleja printed a book that reproduced 449 works attributed to Goya, together with part of his correspondence and Zapater's *"Noticias biográficas"*.

The centenary celebrations in 1928 did much to popularize Goya and spread his fame. Apart from an exhibition in the Prado, several books were published that helped to clear up little-known aspects about his life, including Ezquerra del Bayo's work on Goya and the Duchess of Alba and Sánchez Cantón's study on Goya's visit to Sanlúcar. From a critical-literary point of view, the biographies by the Spanish writers Gómez de la Serna, Eugenio d'Ors and Juan de la Enzina are interesting, as well as publications by the Prado and the National Library on Goya's drawings and etchings. The centenary year marks the beginning of Desparmet Fitz-Gerald's extensive work, which was not finished until 1950.

In 1932 the Spanish Society of Art Friends organized a magnificent exhibition on the *"Antecedentes, coincidencias e influencias del arte de Goya"*. Owing to various circumstances the Catalogue could not be published until 1947, but then it fortunately included by way of a foreword a masterly essay by Lafuente Ferrari on the different problems facing an art critic when trying to assess Goya's personality. This work completed a series of publications commemorating the 200th anniversary of Goya's birth the year before. Exhibitions in the National Library and the Royal Palace, articles in different reviews, lectures in academic sessions, the *"Bibliografía de Goya"* compiled by Ruiz Cabriada and printed by the National Library, as well as a comprehensive study of the tapestry cartoons published by Valentín de Sambricio, all convey sufficient idea of what this bicentenary represented. One of the most interesting documental discoveries was probably that which enabled Sánchez Cantón to imagine *"Como vivía Goya"* using the inventory of his personal effects and documents pertaining to the purchase of his house "La Quinta del Sordo".

The number of newly published works on Goya has not ceased to grow since the middle of the present century and we do not intend burdening the reader with excessive bibliographical notes. The Spanish version (there was a previous French one) of Sánchez Cantón's *"The life and works of Goya"* (1951) can be considered the starting point of a list that includes important monographs. Studies by Lafuente Ferrari on the paintings in the San Antonio de la Florida chapel and on the *Disasters of War*, by Camón Aznar on the *"Disparates"*, by López Rey on the *"Caprichos"*, by Harris on Goya's etchings and lithographs and so many more allow us to assert that few figures in the history of art have been examined so often and from such different angles.

Since 1950 not a year has passed by without a reference to Goya in some part of the world, through exhibitions[9], publication of research work

9. A number of important exhibitions (some of them with magnificent catalogues) have contributed towards keeping alive the public's interest in Goya throughout the world. Without trying to offer an exhaustive list and leaving aside those that dealt exclusively with etchings, since 1950 we could mention the following: Fine Arts Gallery, Bordeaux (1951); Kunsthalle, Basle (1953); Charles V's Palace, Granada (1955); Casón del Buen Retiro, Madrid (1961); Jacquemart-André Museum, Paris (1961-62); Royal Academy, London (1963-64); Johan Maurits van Nassau Foundation, The Hague (1970); L'Orangerie, Paris (1970); Tokyo and Kyoto (1971-72); Pedralbes Palace, Barcelona (1966); Centre Culturel de Marais, Paris (1979); National Museum, Stockholm (1980); Kunsthalle, Hamburg

Goya's letters to his friend Martín Zapater, including telling sketches like this one (no. 56 of the Epistolario), give us a glimpse of Goya from his most human and spirited angle.

or critical studies, printing of new treatises and catalogues of his paintings, drawings or etchings, new biographies or didactic, although often over-imaginative, TV series or films. It is impossible to keep track with the constantly growing bibliography in the second half of this century. In addition to the authors we have referred to so far, we should also mention Xavier de Salas, Nordström, Baticle, E. Helman, Glendinning, E.A. Sayre, Camón, Gállego, etc. and in particular Gudiol and Gassier for their general treatises. When he died in 1976, the Spanish art critic Juan Antonio Gaya Nuño left a *"Bibliografía crítica y antológica de Goya"* (as yet unpublished) that lists over two thousand titles, many of them accompanied by brief commentaries. Since then the list of publications has not ceased to grow. We should add Goya's *"Cartas a Martín Zapater"* compiled by Xavier de Salas and Mercedes Agueda and the *"Diplomatorio"* compiled by Angel Canellas (1981). These few bibliographical notes are intended to demonstrate the unfailing interest that the figure of Goya continues to arouse. Very few artists have attracted the attention of experts in other fields far-removed from the history of art. Such is the case of the Spanish philosopher Ortega y Gasset, who wrote brilliant pages about our master painter[10].

(1980-81); Museo Municipal, Madrid (1982-83); Prado, Madrid (1983); Musées Royaux des Beaux Arts, Brussels (1985); Villa Favorita, Lugano (1986); Saragossa (1986); Madrid (1988), etc. Apart from these, a number of other exhibitions have been held under titles such as "From El Greco to Goya", etc. I doubt that any other artist (with the possible exception of Picasso) has aroused such interest as Goya.

10. Ortega felt particularly attracted by Velázquez and Goya; as far as the latter is concerned, this affinity developed at the end of his life (1950). He explained that he had experienced Goya in the same way as many other Spaniards and Europeans, discovering his "efficacious, penetrating, disturbing" aspect. See the anthology of texts concerning Goya published in the "Revista de Occidente" (Col. "El Arquero", 1966). Outside Spain, the work of Klingender should be mentioned, who from the point of view of a Marxist sociologist tried to reveal through Goya's creations the political, economic and social conflicts of his time. In various exhibitions held in the past few years (e.g. Stockholm, Hamburg, Madrid Municipal Museum) emphasis has been laid on the possible political "message" to be found in Goya's paintings, drawings and etchings.

A LIFE ASTRIDE TWO CENTURIES

Retracing the principal events in the eight long decades of Goya's life is like reliving one of the most intricate periods in the history of mankind. Goya's biography has the value of an eye-witness account of events reaching from the end of the *ancien régime* down to modern times, which he lived mostly as a mere spectator, but on some occasions also as an actor. As we recall his life on the following pages we should however not forget that his paintings, drawings and etchings are invaluable as a mirror of his personality. His life and works cannot be kept apart if we want to reconstruct a true picture of Goya. We hope that this necessarily limited view of his world and creations will help to present him as a man of flesh and blood, with his whims and foibles, his desire to rise in the world and enjoy the creature comforts he had attained, with his occasional fits of defiance and again his surrenders to Fortune's flatteries. If we can reveal Goya's profile as a man, his artistic personality will come out all the clearer.

The great masters of painting (keeping to the Spanish context we have in mind Greco, Velázquez, Goya and Picasso) all reflected the spirit of their time with the help of an uncommonly strong personality and indeed frequently exceeded the limits of their time, creating new forms of expression. Without being inconsistent with their time, they were able to open up new, imaginative horizons in the visual world and each of them in his own way was destined to play an outstanding part in the making and development of contemporary painting.

Goya is a particularly illustrative figure since he embodies the starting point of all the problems of present-day art. On the other hand, historically speaking it is interesting to situate him in those latter decades of the 18th and early decades of the 19th century in which he lived, centered around the French Revolution, because his life illustrates a number of extremely decisive moments. When our painter was born in the little village of

Fuendetodos in Aragón, on March 30th 1746, Philip V was still on the Spanish throne; he died on July 9th of that same year. Goya therefore lived through the reigns of Ferdinand VI (until 1759), Charles III (until 1788), Charles IV (who was forced to abdicate in 1808), Joseph Bonaparte (the "intruder king" during the French invasion from 1808 to 1813) and Ferdinand VII (who died in 1833, five years after Goya). Goya's life is therefore unequally divided over two centuries.

But if we take into account that his genius did not appear at an early age, we can be satisfied that he lived through the years of greatest turmoil in European history (beginning with the French Revolution in 1789) as a mature man. He was approaching his fifties when, in spite of or maybe precisely due to his deafness, his need for communication grew and made him resort to all the means at his disposal: brush, pencil, pen and etching needle. Up till the last decade of the 18th century his personality is best revealed in his correspondence with his friend Zapater. After the illness that caused his deafness in 1793, his reflections on the world around him and his most scathing comments are contained in his drawings and some of his most famous paintings.

Goya during the reign of Ferdinand VI (1746-1759)

It is useful to divide up Goya's life into the reigns of the various kings who succeeded to the Spanish throne after the first Bourbon, Philip V, died when the painter was just over three months old. It is not known exactly why Goya was born in a little village 45 kilometres from Saragossa. His father was a gilder by profession, but had come to live at this place where his wife had relatives who worked on the land. Nothing definite is known about his early childhood either. He is supposed to have gilded a reliquary for the local parish church when he was twelve, but the work no longer exists. A few details have emerged about his ancestors; the latest were published by Xavier de Salas, but they do not shed much light on the subject. By the time Ferdinand VI died in 1759 the gilder and his family must have moved to Saragossa, where the adolescent Goya embarked on his first training as an artist.

Goya during the reign of Charles III (1759-1788)

Sometime around the beginning of Charles III's reign Goya was probably apprenticed to the workshop of José Luzán. Although not an outstanding painter himself, Luzán

was important as a teacher of other artists who later achieved renown at Court. Not only Goya, but also the Bayeu brothers were among his pupils. Goya trained under Luzán until 1763 and it is to be assumed that during these years he came into contact with academic trends because art teaching in Saragossa at the time already ran much along the same lines as at the Academy in Madrid. It is documented in the records of the Royal Academy of San Fernando that Goya was in Madrid on December 4th 1763 to apply for one of the grants awarded by the Academy to young artists who wanted to study in Italy. Goya was not at his best in examinations. The first test consisted in making a pencil drawing on half a demy sheet of the statue of Silenus on show at the Academy. Another entry of January 15th announces that the winner was the painter from Galicia

View of Saragossa, as reproduced on page 11 of Yriarte's book. Goya always kept up his ties with Saragossa and although it may appear a commonplace, everything we know about his character fits perfectly into the picture of a typical Aragonese. His letters to Zapater show how attached he was to his native town where his parents, brothers and sister continued to live and where he paid frequent visits.

The Family of Philip V. *Prado, Madrid. Signed by Louis Michel van Loo in 1743. This group portrait is an interesting record of what royalty was like at the time Goya was born, three years later. Here we see the king, who died a few months after the artist's birth, seated with the future Ferdinand VI (1713-1759) by his side (his reign coincided with Goya's childhood and youth); also, standing on the far right, the future Charles III (1716-1788), with whom Goya was later to start his relationship with the royal family.*

Charles III in hunting attire. *Prado, Madrid. This is the first of Goya's portraits of royalty, painted before he became Court painter under Charles IV. It was probably a commissioned work and several replicas are known. The subject illustrates the king's hunting habits (which he probably pursued more duty-bound than out of true enthusiasm) and the composition reveals Goya's admiration for Velázquez because it is directly related to one of the latter's portraits of Prince Baltasar Carlos.*

Prado Museum, Madrid, Engaving. One of the most ambitious cultural projects undertaken under Charles III was the construction of an enormous building to house his Natural History collection and also serve as a Temple of Science. Unfortunately no documents remain concerning the progress of this building, but it must have been fairly far advanced by 1785. With its long drawn-out Western façade and colonnade it was an attractive addition to the Prado avenue, with the Botanical Gardens next to it. These two projects contributed towards making Juan de Villanueva the most famed architect of the Neo-classical age. Goya was a witness to his work and a personal friend, portraying him in a painting kept in the San Fernando Royal Academy of Arts.

Gregorio Ferro. Two years later Goya experienced his second academic failure. This time he had to submit two history paintings, one prepared in advance and the second "impromptu". He was allowed several months for the first work and two and a half hours for the second. He did not obtain a single vote. The Academy turned its back on him again, but in due course he would have the opportunity of taking his revenge.

Although his visit to Madrid did not produce the artistic success he had dreamed of at the institution that ruled over the arts in the Spanish capital, it is more than probable that Goya nonetheless benefitted

from his contacts with the artistic world of Madrid in the early years of Charles III's reign. On his arrival from Naples, the new king had brought a number of Italian or Italian-trained artists with him. The Rococo was then on its way out and Neoclassicism had taken its place, so it was natural that artists from abroad should come to spread the new style. Due to their influence on Goya some of their names should be remembered here. Corrado Giaquinto had already been working in Madrid from 1753 to 1762. Charles III brought two others, highly reputed in Italy, who were to have a lasting influence on Spanish art. Anton Raphael Mengs, born in Bohemia, was only 33 years old

The Puerta de Alcalá, Madrid, built by Sabatini between 1774-1778. Drawing and lithograph by J. Cebrián. Goya lived through the transformation of Madrid under Charles III and knew the architects who, like Sabatini, were materializing the king's ideas. This gate with its appearance of a triumphal arch was the first of a number of constructions intended to improve the city approaches at the end of the 18th and beginning of the 19th century.

25

when he came to Spain, but his fame commanded respect in the artistic world. The Venetian Giambattista Tiepolo was over 60 when he arrived and his lyrical, finest Baroque style contrasted with the dogmatic Neoclassicism of the younger artist from Germany. Goya must have been keenly interested in the inevitable clash between the two painters. From 1764 to 1769 the Venetian master worked on the decoration of the new Royal Palace in Madrid and the San Pascual church in Aranjuez. The paintings for this church were never hung; their rich colouring was incompatible with Mengs' aesthetic ideals, that laid the accent on draughtsmanship. If the artistic rivalry between Tiepolo and Mengs had its influence on Goya, other events in

The Riot against Esquilache. *Private collection, Paris. On the right:* The maja and the cloaked men. *Prado, Madrid. This strange picture (whose whereabouts are unknown and is reproduced here from an old photograph) refers to a famous event (1766) which was probably witnessed by Goya, who has left us the only known contemporary record on canvas. In his tapestry cartoon* The maja and the cloaked men *there is a clear allusion to the way men hid their identity under cloaks and wide-brimmed hats, like the figure seated on the left. It is a typical Madrid scene and was painted in 1777 for the dining room in the Pardo palace. It has been suggested that the scene is situated in the Casa de Campo park. For unknown reasons contemporary documents refer to it as* A walk in Andalusia.

27

28

During his stay in Italy in 1770-71 Goya took part in a painting contest organized by the Academy of Parma and submitted a work entitled Hannibal crossing the Alps. *This sketch, discovered and published in 1984, could have belonged to that lost work. Its loose handling contrasts with the design and rigorous composition of his* Sacrifice to Pan *that complies with the Classicist norms in vogue at Rome at the time.*

Madrid must also have made an impression on him.

Goya was a first-hand witness to the important renovation work that Charles III was undertaking in Madrid. The Royal Palace that Philip V had begun was now nearing completion. The king was obsessed by the idea of converting Madrid into a worthy capital for his court and promoted a series of notable changes. During his reign the Prado "walk" was turned into a proper avenue with its various fountains, an imposing building designed by the architect Villanueva as a temple of the Sciences and the

Arts before it eventually became the Prado Museum, and the Botanical Gardens. Other new constructions included the Alcalá Gate and the Customs House (now Ministry of Finance). The face of Madrid was gradually changing and even its ground and underground: a sewerage system was set up, streets paved, lighting and street-cleaning services installed, etc. At the same time attempts were made to alter what the king considered bad customs, sometimes even causing disturbances among the people, such as the famous "Riot against Esquilache" in 1766, when the king's unpopular Italian-born Finance Minister Esquilache tried to ban the typical cloaks and wide-brimmed hats worn by men. Goya was most probably not indifferent to these events that upset Madrid life when the reforms were being introduced and it is not difficult to imagine him getting involved with the rioters. He almost certainly supported the royal decree expelling the Jesuits the following year (1767): he painted two pictures to commemorate the event.

At the age of 23, it is not known with what funds, Goya travelled to Italy, where he remained until 1771. These two years were surely beneficial. Sánchez Cantón believed that he might well have returned by land and seen French paintings on the way, to judge by

the influence of some French works on his style. Goya explained in a statement about his stay in Rome that he had "travelled and lived there at his own expense". In 1771 he sent a history painting to the Academy of Parma, obtaining six votes although no prize. At this time he was signing "Goja" and referred to himself as a follower of Francisco Bayeu. The works he painted in Italy reveal the influence of the Italian *settecento*, hesitating between Baroque and Neoclassicist trends. Research by Milicua and the Marquis of Lozoya provided documentary evidence of some pictures: later we shall refer to a portrait and three mythologies painted by Goya at this time.

As mentioned, Goya could have returned to Spain via France, where he was impressed by Simon Vouet's style. He did not return to Madrid this time, but remained in Saragossa where he was commissioned to prepare some preliminary sketches for the Basilica of Our Lady of the Pillar. He spent the next three years in his home area working on a number of commissions,

31

although he visited Madrid at least once, in 1773, to marry Josefa Bayeu, the sister of the Bayeu brothers who were painting at Court[11]. From 1774 on Goya lived in Madrid, working on designs for the Royal Tapestry Manufactory and beginning to paint portraits. By the end of the 1770s he was on the road to fame, despite some setbacks. Apparently he did not always enjoy the best of health: in a letter to his friend Martín Zapater in 1777 he wrote: "Now I am well again; thank God I pulled through". The nature of his illness is unknown; however his convalescence was obviously productive because he began to master the art of engraving and sent several reproductions of Velázquez's works to the king. The following year he described in exaggeratedly excited terms how he had shown some of his paintings to the king and crown prince and princess. At the time he was hoping to be appointed a court painter, a post that was vacant due to Mengs' death.

During the 1780s his artistic career advanced steadily, although petty rivalries sometimes cast a shadow on his satisfaction. An important event was his admission to the Fine Arts Academy of San Fernando in 1780. However this triumph was dimmed when the Saragossa prebendaries raised objections to his preliminary sketches for further works in the Basilica. Goya finally had to give in to pressure and accept Francisco Bayeu's mediation. By this time artistic rivalry had led to antagonism with his brother-in-law.

In contrast with the problems that had cropped up in his home area, Goya had the satisfaction of taking part in an ambitious project that enabled him to compete with some of the most famous artists of his time. On July 25th 1781 he wrote to Zapater: "My friend, the moment has arrived for the most important painting contract to be offered in Madrid because His Majesty has decided to hold a competition to paint pictures for the church of St. Francis the Great and he has deigned to appoint me to take part. The minister is sending a letter to Goicoechea[12] today to show to the

---

11. The Bayeu family, gentry from Bielsa in the Aragonese Pyrenees, was to play a role in Goya's life; his relations with his brothers-in-law were sometimes strained. Ramón Bayeu Solans (born 1700) and María née Subías were the parents of: Francisco (1734-1795), Manuel (1740-1809), Ramón (1746-1793), Josefa (1747-1812) and María (born 1748). The three sons were all painters, the second was also a Carthusian monk.

12. Juan Martín de Goicoechea (1732-1804) is undoubtedly meant, a wealthy businessman who held an important place in the cultural life of Saragossa, participating actively in institutions such as the Economic

wretches who cast doubts on my merits and you will take it where you know it will cause a sensation because there is reason enough: the great Bayeu will also paint his picture and Maella and the rest of the court painters too; this is a proper competition and it seems that God has heard my prayer and I hope that everything will come to a successful end when the paintings are done..."[13]. Goya's letter shows just

Renovation project of the Goyeneche palace, designed by Churriguera, in order to house the Royal Academy of San Fernando. By one of those whims of fate, the institution that had set itself the aim of "restoring good taste" had to make use of a building designed by the Spanish architect after whom an overladen, flamboyant style of Baroque ornamentation known as "Churriguerismo" was named, whose construction however did comply with a certain degree of Classicism. The alterations proposed by Diego de Villanueva in 1772 mainly affected the doorway, windows and socle. Drawing kept in the Academy Museum.

Society of Friends of Aragón and the Academy of San Luis. Goya painted his portrait (of which the original and a replica exist) with an expressive dedication in 1789. He should not be mistaken for Martín Miguel de Goicoechea, who was later to become the father-in-law of Goya's son.
13. The letter closes with the remark "nobody remembers (his brother-in-law) Ramón

how much he was waiting for an opportunity to settle old scores. Although in these circumstances the rivalries must have led to a certain amount of friction, there is no doubt that Goya put all his enthusiasm in his work, which he finished in January 1783, when the various paintings were hung in the church of San Francisco el Grande.

In 1783 Goya received commissions to paint portraits of the *Count of Floridablanca* and the *Infante Don Luis*, which helped him to widen his circle of prospective patrons. He went to great pains to portray the former, a well-known politician and minister, in the centre of a complicated scene that includes a self-portrait of Goya, but the work did not meet with the sitter's approval and Goya's acquaintance with Floridablanca did not last[14]. However,

The Count of Floridablanca. Bank of Spain, Madrid. Goya portrayed José Moñino (1728-1808), 1st Count of Floridablanca, in this composition which probably did not appeal very much to Charles III's famous minister. In one of his letters to Martín Zapater, dated in April 1783, Goya expressed his satisfaction about having achieved a good likeness of the sitter's head, but the general composition is exceedingly stilted. However it dates from a year filled with activity and successes.

his relations with King Charles III's brother did help him in his career. Don Luis is a rather melancholy figure in Spanish history. The king did not want him to marry a woman of royal blood for fear that their possible descendants might contest the right to the throne of the king's son Charles, who had not been born on Spanish soil. He therefore intended appointing his brother Archbishop of Toledo, but the ecclesiastical career did not appeal to the Infante, who finally contracted a morganatic marriage, at the age of 49, with María Teresa Vallabriga, who was then 17[15]. The marriage

Bayeu". It was published by Zapater y Gómez in 1868, but its whereabouts is unknown now. Cf. the notes published by Salas and Agueda in "*Cartas a Martín Zapater*" (1982), page 65.

14. José Moñino, Count of Floridablanca (1728-1808), played an important role in Spanish political life as Public Prosecutor of the Council of Castile. Ambassador in Rome, Minister under Charles III and Charles IV and President (until his death on October 30th) of the Supreme Central Junta that had to stand up to the French invasion. He also faced periods of persecution, as during the 1970s when he was replaced by the Count of Aranda. With regard to the portrait, Floridablanca's only comment in supposed to have been: "We will talk some other time."

15. María Teresa Vallabriga was born in Saragossa in 1759. When her mother died in 1773 she was sent to live with her uncle, the Marquis of San Leonardo, and his wife

stipulations, signed in 1773, included the following terms: "The wife will retain her father's name and coat-of-arms... she must reside outside Madrid, in a province and not in any of the royal seats; the same will apply to her children during their father's lifetime...". It seems interesting to reproduce these brief extracts since the clauses throw light on the narrow circles that Goya was allowed to glimpse. One of his paintings, *The family of the Infante Don Luis*, is reputed in the history of Spanish art to be the first portrait of what was to be the Spanish middle class. The unfortunate prince, who had to resign himself to viewing Madrid from the village of Boadilla del Monte, apart from having to reside in Arenas de San Pedro, in the province of Avila, south of the Gredos mountains, died in 1785 at the age of 58. However, Goya kept up the relationship with his children, the Countess of Chinchón, who married Godoy, Cardinal Luis María de Borbón, later Archbishop of Toledo (his portrait is in the Prado) and the Duchess of San Fernando de Quiroga[16].

In these years Goya built up a considerable circle of patrons and friends who commissioned paintings from him, including important members of the aristocracy, such as the Dukes of Híjar[17] and Osuna. We

---

in Madrid: he was the brother of the 3rd Duke of Berwick and of Liria. Three years later she married the Infante Don Luis. When she was widowed and Charles III died, she was allowed to return to Madrid and finally, in 1792, she moved back to Saragossa.

16. The Countess of Chinchón, who was mag-

---

nificently portrayed by Goya, was María Teresa de Borbón y Vallabriga. She was born in 1779 and died in 1828. It is well known that her marriage was an unhappy one. She finally left Godoy and there is no mention of his name on her tombstone in the palace chapel at Boadilla del Monte. Her brother, Luis María de Borbón y Vallabriga, of whom there is also a portrait by Goya, was born in 1777 and died in 1823, having pursued the ecclesiastical career that his father had rejected; he was a Cardinal and Archbishop of Toledo and is buried in the Cathedral there. The third child of this marriage was María Luisa de Borbón y Vallabriga, who married the Duke of San Fernando de Quiroga; like her sister, she is buried in a beautiful tomb in the palace chapel at Boadilla del Monte, where she is represented embracing her husband's tombstone. Goya kept in contact with her during his stay in Paris. On November 30th 1824 he wrote to her from Bordeaux apologizing for not having paid her a farewell visit before his departure from Paris and sending her, apparently, one or more drawings of three dwarfs he had seen at a fair (Goya: *Diplomatario*, 1981, page 387).

17. The Duke of Híjar must have commissioned a *Virgin of the Pillar appearing to the Apostle St. James*, now kept at Urrea de Gaén (province of Teruel), of which the Prado has a preliminary sketch (see Sánchez Cantón, 1964, page 29). In addition, the portraits of Charles IV and María Luisa by Goya were displayed on the balcony of the Duke's palace in Madrid in 1789 when the King and Queen officially ascended the throne (see Sánchez Cantón: *Los cuadros de Goya en la Real Academia de la Historia*, 1946, page 11).

The Family of the Infante Don Luis.
*Magnani-Rocca Foundation, Parma.
Goya's visits to Arenas de San Pedro
in 1783 and 1784 at the Infante's
invitation (he had been exiled from
Madrid by his brother Charles III) are
reflected in paintings and in his letters
to Martín Zapater. Among the various
works he painted there this one of the
family around a table is particularly
remarkable. The bourgeois
atmosphere of the composition is a
foretaste of 19th-century society.
According to art historian Eduardo
Tejero, the figures are: the Infante
Don Luis, his wife María Teresa de
Vallabriga (who is having her hair
done by her hairdresser Santos
García), their three children (Luis,
later Archbishop of Toledo, María
Teresa, future wife of Godoy, and
María Luisa, later Duchess of San
Fernando de Quiroga, here in her
nurse's arms), two other maids and
three male servants (Juan Miguel de
Aristia, Manuel de Ruylobu and
María Teresa's secretary, Francisco
del Campo). Goya with his back to the
spectator is looking towards all these
figures. It was the first time that a
group portrait like this had been
painted in Spain.*

should attempt to visualize him in the large property that the 9th Duke of Osuna, Pedro Téllez Girón, and his wife, María Josefa Pimentel, Countess of Benavente, had bought in a spot known as "La Alameda" near the village of Barajas. Here, in a spacious park, they built a beautiful Neoclassical palace called *"El Capricho"*, whose rooms were decorated with a number of Goya's paintings, which contributed towards asserting his prestige in aristocratic circles. Although we have no proof, it is not difficult to imagine, as Ezquerra del Bayo did, that it was here at the home of the Osuna family that Goya first met the Duchess of Alba[18].

Art critic Sánchez Cantón considered the year 1785 the starting

The Duke and Duchess of Osuna with their children. *Prado, Madrid. This is a most expressive testimony of Goya's relationship with the Osuna family, for whom he began to work in 1787 on decorations for their palace in La Alameda near Madrid. Some of the children portrayed here sat to Goya again several decades later. The sitters are: María Josefa Alonso Pimentel, Countess-Duchess of Benavente (1752-1834), Pedro Tellez-Girón, 9th Duke of Osuna (1755-1807), and their children Francisco de Borja, future 10th Duke (1785-1820), Pedro, later Director of the Prado and of the Royal Academy of Arts (1786-1851), Josefa Manuela (1783-1838) and Joaquina, later Marquise of Santa Cruz (1784-1851).*

18. A number of works have been published about the Duke and Duchess of Osuna, but we would recommend Antonio Marichalar's *Riesgo y ventura del Duque de Osuna* (Espasa-Calpe, Madrid, 1930) and the Countess of Yebes' *La Condesa-Duquesa de Benavente; una vida en unas cartas* (Espasa-Calpe, Madrid, 1955), which contain a store of documental material and bibliography. The latter work includes interesting references to the palace known as "El Capricho" (page 35 et seq.), as can also be found in Joaquín Ezquerra del Bayo's *La Alameda de Osuna* ("Revista de Archivos, Bibliotecas y Museos", 1926) and *La Duquesa de Alba y Goya* (1928, page 147 et seq.). The 9th Duke of Osuna, Pedro Téllez de Girón, was born in 1755 and died in 1807; his wife, María Josefa Alonso Pimentel, the Countess-Duchess of Benavente, whom he married in 1774, was born in 1752 and died in 1834.

point of Goya's "optimistic period". Indeed, it was the beginning of a run of good luck and successes. At the Academy he was appointed Vice-director of Painting and at Court he was made one of the "King's painters" (1786), along with other less-talented artists such as his brother-in-law Ramón Bayeu.

At the same time he had come into a satisfactory financial position thanks to the income that these posts implied together with his earnings as a portraitist. So we now find Goya installed like a bourgeois gen-

tleman, satisfied with his newly acquired position and able to change his *birlocho* or light carriage (which had caused him an accident that made him hobble for a while) for a four-wheeled berlin carriage drawn by two mules. Thus, with Goya fully occupied in painting not only portraits of distinguished personalities, but also paintings for religious or important financial institutions, like the San Carlos Bank, we reach the end of a period with the death of one of the best kings in Spanish history in December 1788.

this country cannot be regarded without reference to the great crisis that began in Europe with the French Revolution and Napoleon's coronation as Emperor. It is essential to imagine the impression that all these events must have made on Goya's spirit. In these troubled times Goya also underwent crucial changes that had consequences for his life and art.

Goya had always enjoyed the favour of the Prince and Princess who were now King Charles IV and Queen María Luisa and on April

Goya during the reign of Charles IV (1788-1808)

The year 1789 dawned on the first days of a reign that was to be marked by intrigues and misgovernment that filled twenty years of Spanish history; the principal responsible was the royal favourite Manuel Godoy, elevated to the rank of chief minister by the Queen María Luisa, whose lover he was[19]. But the events that took place in

impassionate view of his personality. Born in 1767, Godoy entered the Lifeguards in 1784. A fall from his horse while he was escorting the Queen in 1788 attracted her attention to him. Soon after Floridablanca fell from power in 1792, the new royal favourite occupied his post as chief Minister of State. The ensuing years were marked by his rivalry with the Count of Aranda and Jovellanos and his meddling in important political events in and outside Spain. The first title he obtained was that of Duke of Alcudia in 1792, followed by that of "Prince of the Peace" after signing the Treaty of Basel with France. In 1798 he was officially removed from his post of chief Minister for a period of just under three years, returning to rule over Spanish history until March 19th 1808 when he was overthrown as a result of the Aranjuez uprising. He married the Countess of Chinchón in 1797, but she did not follow him into exile. He accompanied the King and Queen when they left Spain (both died in Italy in 1819) together with his mistress Josefa Tudó, whom he married in 1829, three months after his wife's death. He never returned to Spain and died alone and impoverished in Paris in 1851.

19. The complicated character of Manuel Godoy casts its shadow over the whole of Charles IV's reign from the moment he was raised to the highest posts due to the Queen's infatuation with him. Goya's relations with him should also be taken into account when considering the painter's life. Carlos Seco Serrano wrote an excellent study (*Godoy, el hombre y el político*, Espasa-Calpe, Madrid, 1978) that offers an

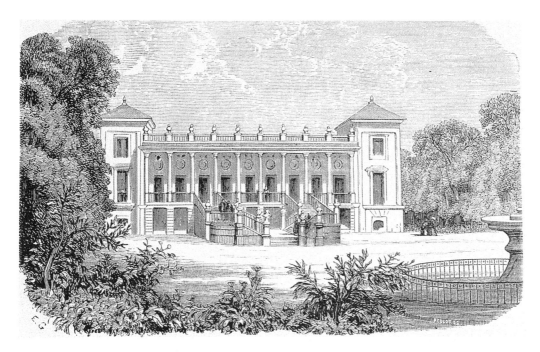

25th 1789 he was appointed Court Painter. On May 6th he participated in "the survey and valuation of the late king's paintings". On July 14th the Bastille was stormed in Paris. During the summer of the following year Goya went to Valencia. He obtained permission to travel there on July 17th, valid for two months, but we do not know what prompted his journey. He is known to have made some paintings and he probably spent most of his spare time hunting in the Albufera area. Maybe he did just what he had described in a letter to his friend Zapater several years before as his ideal state: "Not to have to put up with anything from anybody and go hunting every day". In October he attended the festivities of the Virgin of the Pillar in Sara-

La Alameda de Osuna, *after an etching published in Charles Yriarte's book on Goya. His first acquaintance with one of the most distinguished aristocratic families in Spain, the Osunas, took place in 1787 when he worked on the decoration of the palace that the Duke had just had built in La Alameda near Madrid. El Capricho was the name of this country residence and Goya painted scenes of the parties that were held on the estate, in which he possibly portrayed the Duchess of Alba for the first time.*

41

gossa and at the end of the year he suffered an unspecified illness. During 1791 and 1792 he painted several works and ran into difficulties with the Royal Tapestry Manufactory due to his lack of interest in continuing to produce designs, which on the other hand is understandable considering the rivalries and envy that must have ensued after so many years working together with other artists.

The year 1793 must be considered separately. It was a crucial year because the great breakdown in his health brought about alterations in his character, in his outlook on life and naturally also in his art. His absence from the records of the Academy meetings allows us to deduce that his illness must have lasted about ten months: he did not attend the meetings from September 2nd 1792 until July 11th of the following year. This does not imply that he was bedridden all that time, because he is known to have travelled at least once to Andalusia to convalesce. The documents at our disposal are extremely unclear about his illness and all we can infer is that it was caused by an earlier complaint. Zapater wrote in a letter to the merchant Sebastián Martínez[20], in Cádiz, in whose house

Goya stayed during his illness: "Your esteemed letter of the 5th of this month (January) has caused me the same worries about our dear Goya as your first letter; and since the nature of his illness is of the most fearful, I am heavy-hearted about his possibilities of recovery...". Goya finally won the battle against death, but the price was a permanent deafness that cut him off from the world around him.

The contradictions that we encounter in Goya's life came to a head in the years 1795 to 1797. It is difficult to imagine how a man over fifty suffering from the terrible handicap of his recently acquired deafness could get involved in a youthful passion with the 33-year-

---

20. See Goya: *Diplomatario*, 1981, page 453. Sebastián Martínez was a noteworthy personality from the Rioja region, who offered

Goya hospitality in his house in Cádiz during the artist's serious illness. He held important public posts (Treasurer of the Finance Council and Member of the Royal Council of the Public Treasury) and his successful business enterprises enabled him to get together an outstanding art collection that included "works by Titian, Leonardo da Vinci, Velázquez, Murillo, Alonso Cano and many others, numbering three hundred or more paintings", according to Ponz in his *Viaje de España* (vol. XVIII). Although some of the descriptions this author offers of the paintings should put us on guard against accepting all of the attributions he makes concerning them, his comments reveal the cultured atmosphere that surrounded Goya during his distressing illness. Sebastián Martínez also owned four canvases by Goya, including a splendid portrait dedicated to him, now in the Metropolitan Museum, New York. He died in Murcia in 1800.

Charles IV, *who was born in Naples in 1749 and died there in exile in 1819, reigned in Spain from the death of his father Charles III in 1788 until he was forced to abdicate in 1808. His weak character is admirably reflected in this portrait which Goya painted for Godoy in 1799, together with the one of the Queen, María Luisa, who was also born and died in Italy*

(1751-1819). These two portraits are a foretaste of the fine group portrait of The Family of Charles IV *that he painted a year later. The similarity in dress and mantilla make this painting of the Queen comparable with those of the* Duchess of Alba *(1797; Hispanic Society, New York) and the* Marquise of Santa Cruz *(1799; Louvre, Paris).*

43

old 13th Duchess of Alba, a woman famed for her appeal and coquetries[21]. María del Pilar Teresa Cayetana (plus 29 other names) de Silva y Alvarez de Toledo, baptized in Madrid in 1762, was the only daughter of the Duke of Huescar, the firstborn son of the 12th Duke of Alba (who died before his father) and therefore inherited numerous titles from her grandfather. Since her father died when she was a child and her mother neglected her upbringing, the little Duchess' education left much to be desired. However, she had grown up among simple people and always showed great sympathy for the lower classes. In her childhood she lived not only in Madrid, but also in Piedrahita, north of the Gredos mountains in the province of Avila, where her grandfather had built a handsome palace over the ruins of an old castle. In his *"Memorias de Piedrahita"* a local writer, José Somoza, quoted an old country woman's recollections: "She was brought up here; what a fine heart she had! She was a blessing to this place!... And how pretty she was!

So bright, so happy-natured! And particularly her hair, how beautiful it was! One day I went to see her and she was getting dressed... it's no exaggeration... her hair reached down to her feet... and since she was always so friendly and good-humoured I remember she said to me: My friend, if it embarrasses you to see me naked, I can cover myself with my hair!'".

When she was eleven years old it was decided to marry her to the Marquis of Villafranca. The ceremony took place in 1775[22]. It is difficult to imagine a more ill-suited couple. She was happiest at popular festivities, whereas he enjoyed chamber music. The Duchess' coquettish character made her compete with the Queen in scandalous love affairs. Meanwhile, the Marquis, who maintained correspondence with Haydn, occupied his time organizing concerts with the Infante Don Gabriel. Such was the state of things until 1796 when the Marquis died and Cayetana became a widow. This is the moment to comment on the relations between the Duchess of Alba

21. The brief biography offered here can be enlarged on in Ezquerra del Bayo's well-documented work (1928) and also in the study published by Dr. Blanco Soler (*La Duquesa de Alba y su tiempo*, Madrid, 1949) after exhuming her remains in the San Isidro Cemetery. Sánchez Cantón's account of the relations between Cayetana de Alba and Goya (1951, page 53) can still be considered reliable and valid.

22. José Alvarez de Toledo, Marquis of Villafranca, was born in 1756. He died without an heir and the title passed to his brother Francisco de Borja, Duke of Medinasidonia, whose wife was the lady whom Goya later portrayed with a palette in her hand (in a portrait in the Prado) because she was an amateur painter and member of the Academy of San Fernando.

and Goya which, even if they were intimate, must certainly have been short-lived.

Although so much has been written and still more invented about the supposed love affair between the two, the truth is that there is very little documentary proof to go by. They might have become acquainted at one of the parties held at *"El Capricho"* since the Countess-Duchess of Osuna and the Duchess of Alba are known to have been close friends. It is even possible that Cayetana is portrayed in a painting called *The fall* where Goya recalled an incident that occurred to María

There are no written records that enable us to infer Goya's reaction to the momentous events leading up to the storming of the Bastille on July 14th 1789. However, to understand his personality, the effect that the French Revolution had on life in Spain must necessarily be taken into account. A whole decade later Goya gave vent to his biting criticism of the society of his time in the Caprichos, *followed by other drawings and etchings he made early in the 19th century.*

Josefa Pimentel on a ride. But all this could only prove a superficial friendship. It is pure imagination to try to discover the Duchess in any of the tapestry cartoons. The evidence that suggests the beginning of something more serious is contained in a letter from Goya to his friend Zapater, jokingly dated 1800 in London, but identified by Beroqui and Salas for several reasons as dating from 1794. Goya writes: "You would do better to come and help me paint the lady of Alba who slipped into my studio yesterday to have me paint her face and succeeded...; I also have to paint her full-length..."[23]. This magnificent portrait is the companion piece to that of her husband (in the Prado); it hangs in the Alba family's Liria Palace in Madrid and is dedicated "To the Duchess of Alba, Francisco de Goya. 1795".

After her husband died on June 9th 1796, the Duchess retreated to her country house near Sanlúcar de Barrameda in the famous *Coto de Doñana*, the splendid nature reserve owned by the Medinasidonia family. This place was the setting for the notorious relations between the Duchess and Goya. His stay in Sanlúcar must have been during the last months of 1796 and first months of 1797, although it is also

The Duchess of Alba. Goya's relationship with the house of Alba had an important influence on his life and works. The earliest written mention of this relationship dates from 1974 when Goya wrote to his friend Zapater that the Duchess had slipped into his studio to have him paint her face. After that he painted portraits of the Duke and Duchess and when she became a widow he visited her on her Andalusian estate, where he portrayed her again and presumably had a short-lived romance with her in 1796-97. However, a decade earlier he had worked at the Alameda de Osuna where the Duchess was a frequent visitor. In this portrait, kept at the Alba family residence, the Liria Palace in Madrid, Goya presents Cayetana as an extremely attractive and flirtatious woman; she was 33 years old at the time and only had another seven years to live.

possible that he already visited her in the summer, returning in the autumn. Goya was in poor health in addition to his deafness (those were the grounds he gave to resign from his post as Director of Painting at the Academy on April 30th 1797) and he probably went to the *Coto de Doñana* to convalesce. The Hispanic Society of America in New York has a picture that is an extraordinary pictorial testimony of Goya's attachment to Cayetana. It

---

23. See Goya: *Cartas a Martín Zapater* (1982, pages 225-227).

47

shows the Duchess wearing a mantilla; two rings bear the names *"Goya"* and *"Alba"* and on the ground the words *"Solo Goya"* (Only Goya). There are also two small pictures, whose existence was known but which were only discovered in 1984, that show pleasant scenes at the *Coto*. The first represents *The Duchess' duenna with the negro girl María Luz and the page Luis Berganza*; the boy and girl try to hold back the woman who attempts to escape. In the other picture the *The Duchess of Alba and her duenna* are portrayed, the latter leaning on a stick and holding a crucifix in her right hand, while the Duchess, seen from behind with her splendid hair, seems to be teasing her. This masterly little picture has been purchased for the Prado.

The drawings that Goya made in these months at the *Coto*, many of which he engraved to include them in *"Los Caprichos"*, reflect a tense state of mind and when Cayetana appears in them they seem to reveal the frustrated expectations of a lover, although it will never be possible to fathom their true meaning. The fact that the Duchess is portrayed so often, sometimes with butterfly wings, in the so-called *"Sanlúcar Album"* can be accepted without venturing onto hypothetical ground and interpreting it as a sign of passions and frustrations.

Handwritten report by Goya concerning an amendment to the study programme at the Royal Academy of San Fernando, 1792. This manuscript is interesting in that it reveals Goya's ideas about art training at an important time in his development, shortly before the severe illness that caused his deafness. Prior to this personal crisis, therefore, he was already recommending a kind of artistic freedom that would mean a breakthrough in the Academy's strict rules, in the Neoclassical doctrines imposed by Mengs several decades earlier.

Keeping strictly to fact, we can affirm that Goya's romance in Andalusia, if indeed it was such, was definitely a short-lived affair. After April 1797 their lives went different ways. The Duchess had only another five years to live, which however left her time for several other liaisons. In 1800 the Queen described her maliciously in a letter to Godoy as "gone to rack and ruin". She died on July 23rd 1802 and it was rumoured that she had been poisoned[24].

---

24. When her remains were examined, as reported by Dr. Blanco Soler (see note 21 above), no traces of arsenic were discovered in the bones that were analysed.

Exᵐᵒ Sᵒʳ

Cumpliendo por mi parte con la orden de V.E. para que cada uno de nosotros exponga lo que tenga por conveniente sobre el Estudio de las Artes, digo: Que las Academias, no deben ser privativas, ni servir mas que de Auxilio a los que libremente quieran estudiar en ellas, desterrando toda sugecion servil de Escuela de Niños, preceptos mecanicos, premios mensuales, ayudas de costa, y otras pequeñeces que envilecen, y afeminan un Arte tan liberal y noble como es la Pintura; tampoco se debe preffisar tiempo de que estudien Geometria, ni perspectiva para vencer dificultades en el dibujo, que este mismo las pide necesariamente a su tiempo a los que descubren disposicion, y talentos, y quanto mas adelantados en el, mas facilmente consiguen la ciencia en las demas Artes, como tenemos los exemplares delas que mas han subido en este punto, que no los cito por ser cosa tan notoria. Dare una prueba para demostrar con hechos; que no hay reglas en la Pintura, y questa opresion, u obligacion servil de hacer estudiar, o seguir a todos por un mismo camino, es un grande impedimento a los Jovenes que profesan este arte tan dificil, que toca mas en lo Divino que ningun otro, por significar quanto Dios ha criado. El que mas se haya acercado podra dar pocas reglas delas profundas funciones del entendimiento que para ello se necesitan, ni decir en que consiste haber sido mas feliz tal vez en la obra de menos cuidado, que en la de mayor esmero, que profundo, é impenetrable arcano se encierra en la

imitacion de la divina naturaleza, que sin ella nada hay bueno, no solo en la Pintura (que no tiene otro oficio que su puntual imitacion) sino en las demas ciencias!

Anibal Carche, resucitó la Pintura que desde el tiempo de Rafael estaba decaida; con la liberalidad de su genio, dió á luz mas discipulos, y mejores que quantos Profesores ha habido, dejando á cada uno correr por donde su espiritu le inclinaba, sin preciar á ninguno á seguir su estilo, ni metodo, poniendo solo aquellas correcciones que se dirigen á conseguir la imitacion dela verdad, y asi se ven los diferentes estilos, de Guido, Guarchino, Andrea, Sacqui, Lanfranco, Albano &ᵃ.

No puedo dejar de dar otra prueba mas clara. Delos Pintores que hemos conocido de mas abilidad y que mas se han esmerado en enseñar el camino á sus fatigados utiles (segun nos han dado á entender) ¿quantos discipulos han sacado? en donde estan esos progresos? estas reglas? este metodo? ¿delo que han escrito se ha conseguido otro adelantamiento mas que interesar á los que no son, ni han podido ser Profesores, con el objeto de que realzasen mas sus obras, y darles amplias facultades para decidir aun á presencia delos inteligentes de una tan sagrada ciencia que tanto estudio exige (aun delos que han nacido para ella) para entender y discernir lo mejor!

Me es imposible expresar el dolor que me causa el ver correr tal vez la licenciosa, ó eloquente pluma (que tanto arrastra al no profesor) incurrir en la debilidad de no conocer á fondo la materia que esta tratando; ¿que escandalo no causara, el oir despreciar la naturaleza en comparacion de las Estatuas Griegas, por quien no conoce ni lo uno,

ni lo otro, sin atender á la mas pequeña parte de la naturaleza confunde, y admira á los que mas han sabido! ¿que Estatua ni forma se halla, que no sea copiada de la Divina naturaleza? ¿y por mas excelente Profesor que sea el que la haya copiado, dejara de decir a gritos puesta á su lado, que la una es obra de Dios, y la otra de nuestras miserables manos? El que quiera apartarse, y enmendar la sin buscar lo mejor de ella, dejará de incurrir en una manera reprehensible monotona de Pinturas, de modelos de Yeso, como ha sucedido á todos los que puntualmente lo han hecho? Parece que me aparto del fin primero, pero nada hay mas preciso, si hubiera remedio, para la actual decadencia de las Artes sino que se sepa que no deben ver arrastradas del poder, ni de la sabiduria de las otras ciencias, sino governadas del merito de ellas, como siempre ha sucedido quando ha habido grandes Imperios florecientes: entonces cesan los desprecios extraños, y nacen los prudentes amadores, que aprecian, veneran, y animan á los que sobresalen, proporcionandoles obras en que puedan adelantar mas en ingenio, ayudandoles con el mayor esfuerzo á producir todo quanto su disposicion promete, esta es la verdadera proteccion delas Artes, y siempre se ha verificado que las obras han creado los hombres grandes. Por ultimo Sᵒʳ yo no encuentro otro medio mas eficaz de adelantar las Artes, ni creo que le haya, sino el de premiar y proteger al que despunte en ellas; el de dar mucha estimacion al Profesor que lo sea; y el de dejar en su plena libertad correr el genio delos Discipulos que quieren aprenderlas, sin oprimirlo, ni poner medios para torcer la inclinacion que manifiestan á este, ó aquel estilo, en la Pintura.

He dicho mi parecer, cumpliendo con el encargo de V.E. mas no es mi mano la que governa la pluma como yo quisiera para dar a entender lo que

comprendo, espero que V.E. lo disculpará, pues la he tenido ocupada toda mi vista deseando conseguir el fruto delo que estoy tratando.

Madrid 14 de Octubre de 1792.

Exᵐᵒ Sᵒʳ
Franᶜᵒ. de Goya

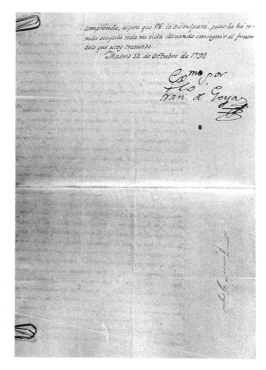

This story calls for a few considerations. In her will Cayetana left a pension of 10 *reales* a day to Goya's son, which seems to reveal affection over and above a mere sinful love affair. And the fact that Goya prepared some sketches for her pantheon does not necessarily mean more than a tribute to the memory of a woman who might have been the cause of a fleeting passion. We can leave it to the reader's imagination to add the details of this friendship or love. Maybe it is better for history and art that the most romantic episode in Goya's biography should leave so many unanswered questions. Elías Tormo once wrote that a jury would probably find him guilty, but a judge would have to decide his acquittal. May the final sentence remain unpronounced and the enigma of those words "Only Goya" live on in all their poetic worth.

From a material point of view Goya's life in this last decade of the century can be termed prosperous. Socially and economically he had a position, as can be inferred from documents concerning a house he bought in 1803 and the wedding of his son Javier, whom he helped financially in 1805 and 1806. The large number of portraits he painted in these years must have provided him with a steady source of income. References to him in the Queen's correspondence show that

Melchor Gaspar de Jovellanos. Prado, Madrid. Goya was not really an intellectual himself, but he lived in contact with some of the most outstanding and enlightened intellectuals of 18th-century Spain. Several records bear witness to his cordial and close relationship with Jovellanos whom he portrayed twice. This portrait dates from 1798, a very creative year for Goya.

he was held in esteem. However, Goya was unimpressed by courtly flattery and must have felt ideologically out of place in these circles that acclaimed him. Charles IV's court had sunk to unknown levels of degeneration owing to the infamous conduct of Godoy, who had risen from the ranks of the Royal Guard to be created successively Duke of Alcudia and "Prince of the Peace" after his "victory" in the ridiculous military campaign against Portugal known as the "War of the Oranges" (from the bough of oranges that Godoy sent to the Queen from Olivenza, "conquered" by the Spanish troops). The internal crisis of the Spanish monarchy must be regarded in the light of external events that reach from the French Revolution to the rise of Napoleon to First Consul and then Emperor. As far as Goya is concerned, he should be considered in the context of his circle of friends

Manuel Godoy. *Royal Academy of San Fernando, Madrid. During the last decade of the 18th century and the early years of the 19th century Spanish history was dominated by the controversial figure of Godoy, whom Goya depicted in a masterly fashion in this portrait that recalls the so-called "War of the Oranges" against Portugal, in which Godoy hoped to become King of the Algarve. Painted in 1801, this portrait is the most revealing graphic record of the "Prince of the Peace", who at the time was married to the daughter of the Infante Don Luis, the Countess of Chinchón.*

The dream of reason brings forth monsters. *Preparatory sketch for etching no. 43 of the* Caprichos. *Prado, Madrid. This is one of two sketches that Goya made before he etched the same-named* Capricho. *This sepia drawing entitled "Dreams" includes an expressive caption that did not appear on the copper etching-plate, where on the other hand a host of vampires and owls hover around the artist lost in his dream world. This plate was originally intended to be the frontispiece of the* Caprichos, *but in the end Goya chose a self-portrait of himself in a serene mood for the title page.*

outside the Court, in particular literary men and intellectuals concerned with social and economic affairs, such as the politician Jovellanos[25].

The contradictions of this period are best reflected in the very different aspects of Goya's work. On the one hand we have the great visionary, not only in the etchings known as *"Los Caprichos"*, but also in the little pictures of witches painted in 1798. But this same year, on

25. Gaspar Melchor de Jovellanos (1744-1811) was virtually the same age as Goya, but died 17 years before the painter. The relations between the two men throw light on Goya's connections with other leading figures of Spanish Enlightenment. These relations have been studied in detail by Edith Helman (*Jovellanos y Goya*, 1970) and are also reflected in some of the subjects of the *Caprichos*. Jovellanos was born in Gijón, Asturias, and engaged in literary pursuits in his youth, but he is best known for his subsequent political activity. During Charles III's reign he was a Justice of the Peace in Seville (1767) and a magistrate in Madrid (1778). He also drew up ordinances for the creation of the Bank of San Carlos and wrote important treatises on the Fine Arts (1782). During Charles IV's reign he fell out of favour with Godoy and for a while he was banished to Asturias and later imprisoned in Majorca, alternating with fruitful intervals in Madrid. In the face of great difficulties he continued to work on important projects that enhanced his prestige, such as his *Informe sobre la Ley agraria* (1794). The magnificent portrait that Goya painted of Jovellanos in 1797, on view in the Prado, bears witness to their friendship. For a biography of Jovellanos, see Juan Antonio Cabezas: *Jovellanos, el fracaso de la Ilustración* (Silex, Madrid, 1985).

the other hand, he carried out the extraordinary series of frescoes in the San Antonio de la Florida chapel, with an extremely loose technique that reveals the changes that had taken place in his art since he had worked on the ceiling of the Basilica in Saragossa. In his portraits we can also discover great innovations, as can be appreciated in important examples on show in the Prado, first and foremost *"The Family of Charles IV"*.

The reign of Charles IV came to an end on March 19th 1808 with the so-called "Revolt at Aranjuez", which led to the fall of Godoy and the king's abdication in favour of Prince Ferdinand, who thus succeeded in his conspiracy against his father, although only temporarily. Let us imagine Goya as a silent eye-witness to all these events, in which the people, who had most seriously suffered the effects of years of misgovernment, were a mere plaything in the hands of stronger forces. The invasion of the Peninsula by French troops was the beginning of one of the greatest upheavals in modern Spanish history: the Peninsular War.

Goya at the time of Joseph Bonaparte (1808-1813)

Any analysis of this period, which begins with the events of May 2nd

1808 in Madrid, must take into account not only the significance of French troops putting an end to Spain's political independence, but also the enormous ideological implications accompanying these troops. This is what made those dramatic years particulary controversial and full of contradictions. At heart the overwhelming majority of Spaniards had to oppose the foreign invasion. But in enlightened and progressive circles the political ideas born of the French Revolution, including all the modifications introduced by the Napoleonic Em-

The Charge of the Mamelukes in the Puerta del Sol. *Prado, Madrid.*
This is the most vivid record of the events of May 2nd 1808. Although the picture was painted after the war, it may be that Goya was reliving a scene he witnessed personally and possibly even sketched at the time (Cf. Sketch in the Duke of Villahermosa's Collection, Madrid) with a very vague background which is difficult to recognize as the famous square prior to its remodellation in the 19th century.

As well as in Goya's masterly canvases the May 2nd uprising against the French troops was recorded visually in lithographs like this one that reproduces the popular interpretation of those events. This engraving by Urrabieta Vierge depicts the outbreak of the tragic revolt in front of the Royal Palace with a bold technique that in some way recalls that of our painter.

pire, opened up new prospects for the history of Spain. The corruption that had characterized Charles IV's court, in spite of a few attempts at enlightenment (some admittedly even due to Godoy himself), was sufficient justification for a minority to place high hopes in the new régime. These were known as *"afrancesados"* (Frenchified). Their degree of collaboration with the French ranged from an attitude of servile flattery to a position that made a clear distinction between accepting ideological principles and submitting to dishonourable situations.

All these considerations are necessary in order to situate Goya in the hectic atmosphere in which Spain was immersed during the French invasion. As soon as the Bourbons had abdicated Napoleon handed Spain over to his brother Joseph Bonaparte, who managed to maintain himself on the throne with difficulty for five years. It is well known that Goya avoided a rupture with the "intruder king" just as he refrained from priding himself on having collaborated with him, although many of his intellectual friends openly did so. He merely complied with the rules laid down by the new régime, accepting as a member of the Royal Academy the

The abdication of Charles IV to Napoleon. *Handbills preserved in the Madrid Municipal Museum reflect, although with poor means and technique, popular feeling about the events of 1808, as here the king's disgraceful abdication in Bayonne.*

57

"project" established by the monarch. He was awarded the "Royal Order of Spain" in 1811 (known disparagingly as "Order of the Aubergine" owing to its colour) and he even painted Joseph I's portrait, which in equity can be considered justifiable since he continued to hold the post of Court Painter and, like Maella, draw his official salary. He also portrayed the king in a medallion now hidden under several layers of paint in a work called *Allegory of Madrid with Joseph I* commissioned by the Madrid City Council.

Apart from these few details, Goya lived discreetly in the shadow at the intruder king's court. There is very little information about his activities during this period, but a revealing document of his personal circumstances, published by Sánchez Cantón, is the inventory of his belongings contained in his house in the Valverde street, drawn up when his wife died in 1812. Unfortunately the books in his library are not specified, as this would be an invaluable help to assessing his cultural background. However, the furniture, valuables, clothing and paintings, both his own and those by other artists, are all listed in detail. On the whole the inventory reflects the background of a man in a comfortable position, in spite of the economic difficulties he alleged after the war to justify his conduct during those years.

Allegory of the City of Madrid. Museo Municipal, Madrid. It is difficult to reconcile the idea that the same artist who painted the tragic May 2nd uprising was capable of contriving this complicated allegory where a portrait of the intruder king, Joseph Bonaparte, was meant to take pride of place in the large oval medallion. Goya depicted this kind of allegory on other occasions. The King's face was later made to disappear from the medallion, as may be supposed, and after several re-paintings was finally replaced by the historic date and the picture was given its present-day title.

The works that he produced in this period are mainly painted to satisfy his need to express his own personal emotions and ideas. These include extremely imaginative small pictures with frightening scenes of the Inquisition (his friend the canon Llorente[26] had access to secret

___

26. Juan Antonio Llorente (1756-1822) was born in Rincón de Soto, Logroño. In his capacity as Secretary of the Court of the Holy Office (i.e. Inquisition) between 1789 and 1791, he compiled a wealth of material concerning the Inquisition which he used to document his writings, such as his *Historia crítica de la Inquisición*. He served under Joseph Bonaparte. Goya must have painted his portrait about 1811; the painting belongs to the Museum of Sao Paulo (Brasil). He went into exile in 1813, returned to Spain during the 3-year constitutional period (1820-23) and died in Madrid.

archives and presumably passed details on to him), lunatic asylums, witches and flagellants' processions; on other occasions he painted grotesque scenes like *The burial of the sardine* (representing a popular ceremony associated with the end of Carnival and beginning of Lent) or tragic ones relating to specific episodes of the war. The impression of the events of May 2nd and 3rd probably inspired him to sketch preliminary studies for the large-scale paintings which he completed six years later. The hallucinating figure of Napoleon probably moved him to imagine the *Colossus* or *Panic*. But Goya reached the height of his expressiveness and sincerity when he reconstructed scenes of ambushes and killings in the drawings known as *The Disasters of War*, which he worked on, including the engravings, until about 1820.

Because they are of different extraction. With reason or without it. *Etchings nos. 61 and 2 of the* Disasters of War. *Between 1808 and 1822 Goya produced a large number of drawings and etchings that reflect in a most merciless manner the situation during the Peninsular War and the ensuing Absolutist era under Ferdinand VII. The* Disasters *reveal an undercurrent of biting criticism that is sometimes directed not only at the invading forces, but also at the social groups responsible for so much bloodshed and misery. In order to fully appreciate the value of these works as a testimony we should also consider other drawings of which he did not make etchings. The guiding theme of all these works is that of misery, stark violence and death.*

Goya during the reign of Ferdinand VII (1814-1828)

Goya turned 68 a month before Ferdinand VII made his triumphant entry in Madrid on May 7th 1814. Shortly before, in Valencia, the king had abolished the liberal (i.e. French-inspired) Constitution worked out by the patriots in Cádiz in 1812. Several weeks earlier our painter had expressed

his "ardent desire to perpetuate with his brush the most memorable and heroic episodes of our glorious uprising against the tyrant of Europe...". At the same time he referred to his state of absolute need in order to apply for an allowance from the public treasury. Later, thanks to his prestige, he was exonerated in an action brought against him for political responsibility. He was allowed to return to his post as Court Painter, although this did not imply enthusiasm on his part for the new king. The var-

Con razon ò sin ella.

ious portraits that he painted of Ferdinand VII (two of them are in the Prado) were not royal commissions and their features come close to appearing caricatures of the king. Approaching the age of seventy, Goya once again took refuge in his own inner world of visions, letting his imagination fly, although he continued to work as a portraitist. He experienced the ups and downs of politics for about ten years, beginning with the persecution of the *"afrancesados"*, including some of his own friends, and later, in 1820, the reaction against absolutist rule following a *pronunciamiento* by a battalion commander called Riego in Cabezas de San Juan[27]. He more than probably welcomed the ensuing constitutional period with great enthusiasm, but must also have shared the disappointment of many Spaniards over the lack of stability and the disorders that prevailed during these three years. Foreign intervention became inevitable and finally

Ferdinand VII in his State robes. Prado, Madrid. Goya virtually ceased to work as Court Painter after completing The Family of Charles IV *in 1800. It is not known whether the Queen was displeased with that famous painting that made the lack of union between the members of the royal family all too evident. The fact is that after the Peninsular War Goya painted several portraits of the new king as private commissions, not in his capacity as Court Painter. In all of them the king is portrayed with a veracity bordering on caricature. Goya's estrangement from Court circles after 1814 was complete, although he retained his post at Court.*

French troops, popularly known as the "Hundred thousand sons of St. Louis", were dispatched to put an end to this constitutional period, while Riego died at the gallows.

On February 27th 1819 Goya had bought a piece of land of over 14 *fanegas* (almost 23 acres) with a house on the far bank of the Manzanares river near St. Isidore's hermitage. This was the famous *"Quinta del Sordo"* where he probably spent the summer months during the last years he lived in Madrid. He covered the walls of two of the rooms with the remarkable *Black Paintings*, whose subject-matter

---

27. Rafael del Riego was a battalion commander who led a pronunciamiento in pro of the Constitution of 1812 in a village near Seville on January 1st 1820. This sparked off a movement that spread through Spain in a matter of weeks, initiating the so-called Constitutional period, in which King Ferdinand VII was forced to solemnly swear allegiance to the Constitution (July 9th 1820). After various vicissitudes this period culminated in the restoration of absolutist rule on October 1st 1823 and Riego's execution on November 7th.

and vigorously Expressionistic-style technique represent the most important self-revelation of Goya's old age.

Spain's return to absolutist rule must have filled Goya with misgivings and anxiety. As a result he took steps to secure his possessions, such as making over the *"Quinta"* to his grandson Mariano[28]. He himself took refuge in a friend's house (José Duaso[29]) for several months

and when the persecution of the liberals began to calm down, in May 1824, he requested permission to leave Spain pretexting a thermal cure at Plombières in the Vosges. The king granted this permission on May 30th and by June 27th Goya was already in France, not at the famous spa, but in Bordeaux.

We have accounts of Goya's stay in Bordeaux thanks to letters written by an exiled friend, the author Leandro Fernández de Moratín[30], who described the artist's arrival: "He arrived indeed, old, deaf, slow in movements and weak, not know-

28. Goya's grandson Pío Mariano de Goya y Goicoechea was a rather unusual figure. Born in 1806, a year after his father Javier's marriage to Gumersinda Goicoechea, he was 22 at the time of his grandfather's death and 48 when his father died. He married Concepción Mariategui, the daughter of the chief municipal architect of Madrid, who was an amateur singer. His liberal ideas did not prevent him from trying to obtain the title of Marquis of Espinar, whose rights had been granted to him by José Maestre. He purchased former church properties that had been secularized, but misfortunate investments and possibly gambling debts caused him financial ruin. After being widowed in 1859, he re-married and had two daughters, Luisa and Francisca. During the last years of his life (until his death in 1874) he lived in various villages in the mountainous area north of Madrid around Somosierra. His biography has been traced by Lafuente Ferrari (1947, page 95).

29. His life is known thanks to a *Biografía del Doctor Don José Duaso y Latre, Caballero de la Real y distinguida orden de Carlos III, Capellán de Honor de S.M. y Juez de su Real Capilla, etc.* (Madrid, 1850), quoted by Sánchez Cantón in *Goya refugiado* (1954). Born in 1775 in a village near Huesca (Aragonese Pyrenees), in 1799 Duaso was a priest. Among other posts he

held that of chief Army chaplain during the Peninsular War and saved the treasures in the Royal Palace chapel. In 1813 he was a member of the regional Aragonese parliament and belonged to the Spanish Royal Academy. After the Constitutional period was over, he enjoyed the King's favour, which enabled him to protect a number of friends and fellow Aragonese. He died in 1849. At the age of 78 Goya painted an excellent portrait of Duaso, which was in a private collection in Madrid until it was purchased by the State in 1969 for the Museum in Seville. Núñez de Arenas believed that Goya took refuge in Duaso's house in 1824 (cf. Fauque-Villanueva, 1982, page 33).

30. Leandro Fernández de Moratín (1760-1828) is well-known in the history of Spanish literature. His correspondence and two portraits by Goya dated in 1799 and 1824 (in the Academy of San Fernando and the Museum of Bilbao) reveal his close friendship with the artist (see Edith Helman's excellent study: *The Younger Moratín and Goya: on duendes and brujas*, 1959, pages 151-181, and also Moratín's correspondence).

ing a word of French and without a servant (which is what he needs most), but content and eager to see the world. He spent three days here and twice came to lunch with us as if he were a young disciple. I have pleaded with him to return by September and not get bogged down in Paris, where winter would be his end..."[31]. The letter reflects perfectly Goya's lively temperament and curiosity to see Paris, the city where the foundations of contemporary art were being laid. By chance Goya arrived there just as the new, free technique, with its

La Quinta del Sordo *This lithograph reproduced by Yriarte in his book on Goya is one of the few illustrations that exist of the country house that Goya purchased near the River Manzanares. The long façade visible through the trees makes it easy to imagine the two large rooms, one on each floor, where Goya painted his impressive murals known as the "Black Paintings".*

---

31. This letter and others are to be found in Moratín's *Epistolario* published by René Andioc (Ed. Castalia, Madrid, 1973).

bold brushwork, was about to triumph, upheld by Delacroix against all the previous academic trends. Curiously enough, for the Spanish authorities this visit to Paris was ground for suspicion. The Minister of the Interior sent out an order "that it be ascertained whether he makes suspicious contacts that might be undesirable considering his position at the Spanish Court" and adding that "he should therefore be closely but discreetly observed". A 20th-century exile, Núñez de Arenas, who researched into Goya's life in France, described the atmosphere that he probably lived in Paris: on the one hand, the Spaniards, most of them political exiles, and on the other the Louvre, the Palais de Luxembourg and the great exhibition opened on King Louis XVIII's namesday, August 25th[32].

By mid-September Goya was back in Bordeaux and installed himself in the house of Leocadia Weiss and her two children, Guillermo and Rosarito[33]. Goya's relations with

A manola: Doña Leocadia Zorrilla. Prado, Madrid. This figure leaning on a rocky mass topped by a strange iron adornment has been identified as Leocadia Zorrilla, the woman who looked after Goya during the last years of his life, with whom he possibly had a somewhat dubious relationship. The identification is probably correct since the title figures in Brugada's inventory. In general this painting reminds us that the original subject-matter of the so-called "Black Paintings" was of a pleasant nature, landscapes predominating, until disturbing topics were painted over or into the original murals (as X-rays subsequently revealed).

menacing humour". However, he recognized Rosario as his legitimate daughter when she was born on October 2nd 1814, although there are suspicions that Goya's affection for the child may have been motivated by very personal reasons. A friend of Goya, the painter Antonio Brugada, who made an inventory of the paintings in the "Quinta" in 1828, identified one of the female figures depicted in a painting on the ground floor as "the Leocadia". When Leocadia settled in Bordeaux in 1824 with her children and Goya, it must be presumed that her marriage had definitively broken down. Isidoro Weiss died in 1850 and his wife (who sank into poverty after Goya's death) six years later. Rosario, who made drawings and lithographs, died in 1843, while Leocadia's son Guillermo, after seeing military service in France, constructed pianos or simply furniture and lived to a ripe old age. The Marquis of Saltillo and Núñez de Arenas compiled the details about this family, which were used by Xavier de Salas (see Sánchez Cantón and Salas, 1963, chapter on *Doña Leocadia y su familia*, pages 83-86. See also Fauque-Villanueva, 1982, page 100 et seq.).

32. See the interesting chapter entitled *La suerte de Goya en Francia. Manojo de noticias* in Núñez de Arenas' work (1963, pages 207-242).
33. Leocadia Zorrilla married Isidoro Weiss in 1807; he was a merchant of German extraction, but had been born in Madrid in 1785. The couple's happiness must have been short-lived because documents of 1811 and 1812 show that he accused his wife of "infidelity, immoral behaviour and misconduct, in addition to an arrogant and

this woman fill the last chapter of his biography and give us a glimpse of not always pleasant aspects of his private life. It is more than probable that their relations had begun many years earlier in Madrid. In France, according to her own declarations, she patiently endured the aged artist's bad moods, while he concentrated his affection on her little daughter, Rosarito, whom he taught to draw. In the meantime his leave of absence had expired and he had to request a new one, this time for a supposed cure at Bagnères spa. Moratín wrote in April 1825: "With his 79 years and his aches and pains, he knows neither what he wants nor what he expects. He likes the town and the countryside, the climate, the food, and he enjoys his independence and his peace. Since he arrived here he has suffered none of the complaints that troubled him back there, but all the same he sometimes gets it into his head that he has a lot to do in Madrid and if they allowed him he would be off on a wretched mule, with his cap and cloak, his wooden stirrups, his wineskin and his saddle-bags".

Various authors like Sánchez Cantón, Lafuente, Núñez de Arenas and others quote a wealth of anecdotes about the last two years of Goya's life, that show the 80-year-old artist's surprisingly vigorous temperament. "He paints like

Goya with his physician Dr. Arrieta. Minneapolis Institute of Arts. His recurring bouts of ill-health played an important part in Goya's life. Some left a definite mark on his work. His illness in 1819, which this painting refers to, fits into a period in which he also executed his "Black Paintings", although in fact the grim, pathetic mood of those works is due to other influences. Goya's inventive talent is revealed in this unusual composition, including one of his last self-portraits, with strange dim figures apparently watching in the background.

wildfire, without even stopping to correct...". In May 1826 he managed to make a quick trip to Madrid in order to obtain, on June 17th, his retirement as Court Painter with a full pension and permission to return to France. It may be observed how careful he was not to cause a breach with the king, thus retaining benefits and privileges. And so we reach the last months of his life, passing over suggestions that he might have travelled again to Madrid and Paris in the month of September. In March 1928 he was impatiently awaiting his son, daughter-in-law and grandson. Mother and son arrived on the 28th, but Javier had to postpone his visit;

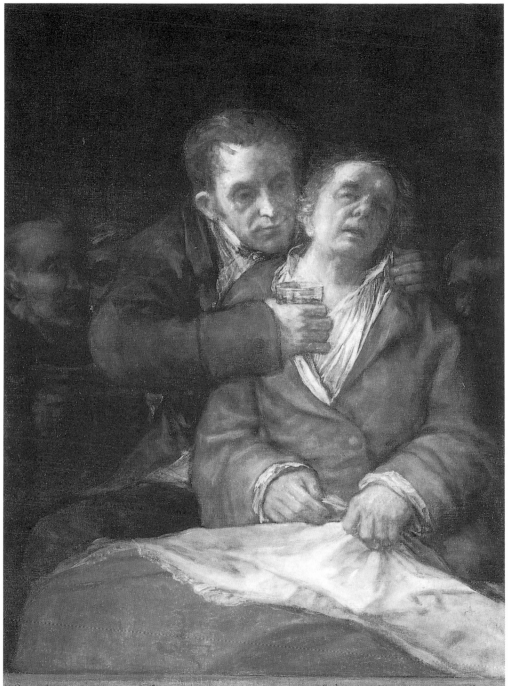

Goya agradecido á su amigo Arrieta: por el acierto y esmero con q. le salvó la vida en su aguda y peligrosa enfermedad, padecida á fines del año 1819 á los setenta y tres de su edad. Lo pintó en 1820.

Goya was ill when his son arrived, having suffered a stroke on April 2nd. He died early on the 16th, soon after his 82nd birthday.

To complete the picture the unpleasant problems must be recalled that cropped up between the painter's family and Leocadia and left her in an almost penniless state. The story of Goya's descendants, his bourgeois son Javier and his headstrong grandson Mariano, is a prosaic one and has been admirably told by the Marquis of Saltillo and Lafuente Ferrari. And finally the adventures of his remains should also be mentioned. He was buried in the same grave as his son's father-in-law, who had died in Bordeaux in 1825. The remains were put together and when Goya's body was exhumed to be transferred to Madrid, one of the skulls was missing. But whose...? Had Goya's really been stolen, as rumours had it, in a romantic fit by the painter Dionisio Fierros? The truth is that the events that occurred up till 1919 when Goya's remains were finally laid to rest in the San Antonio de la Florida chapel in Madrid are merely a repetition of the strange fate that befell the remains of other great Spanish painters. In this, like Greco and Velázquez, Goya was no exception[34].

"I am still learning" Pencil drawing. Prado, Madrid. Famous Goya experts, like Sánchez Cantón and Lafuente Ferrari, considered this old man with his long white hair and beard, leaning on two sticks, to symbolize the end of the artist's life cycle, as if it were a self-portrait of his restless spirit. The drawing figures in one of the Bordeaux albums (G) and therefore dates from the last years of his life.

The man Goya

The story of his life inevitably raises the question of what Goya was like in character. For this purpose the most sincere documents at our disposal are letters to his friend Martín Zapater and drawings, in particular those he did not engrave in order to avoid them being published. His letters sometimes include revealing sketches, like the amusing self-caricature in profile with the words "This is the way I am" in the famous letter, playfully dated in London in 1800, in which he tells Zapater how the Duchess of Alba let herself into his studio.

---

34. Details about Goya in France and the return of his remains to Spain can be found in Fauque-Villanueva's work (1982).

It would exceed the scope of this book to examine these letters in detail to obtain a picture of Goya's personality that would bring us up to the last years of the 18th century. However, the conclusion that may be drawn from them is that they reveal a much more normal personality than the man described by Yriarte in 1867, quoted by Tubino: "Quick-tempered, violent, hot-headed, uncontrollable, incapable of submitting to any restraint or accepting any rules, Goya often risked his life for a word, faced the greatest dangers and made enemies among the powerful..."[35].

The main feature that stands out in Goya's correspondence is his devotion to his friends. He certainly had many good friends, but none as close as Martín Zapater; his attachment to him sometimes appears to us exaggerated in his effusiveness. His large circle of friends included the liberal merchant from Cádiz Sebastián Martínez, the Aragonese businessman Goicoechea, the scholar Llaguno, the art historian Ceán Bermúdez, the politician Jovellanos, José Duaso, in whose house he took refuge during the absolutist persecution, the architects Ventura Rodríguez and Villanueva, actors like Maíquez, authors like Moratín and many others[36].

When considering the world of Goya's personal affections, we cannot overlook his own family, although his references to his wife Josefa do not allow us to assess his feelings towards her. However, there is no doubt about his fondness for his son Javier and especially his

---

35. See Lafuente-Ferrari's comments (1947, pages 27-28).

36. Regarding the figures of Martín Zapater, Sebastián Martínez, Juan Martín Goicoechea, Jovellanos, Duaso and Moratín, see notes 2, 12, 20, 25, 29 and 30 above. Eugenio Llaguno y Amirola (1724-1799) was one of the most distinguished scholars of his time; he held important posts in the Royal Academy of History and was also Minister of Justice. His name is associated with that of Juan Agustín Ceán Bermúdez (1749-1829), who edited Llaguno's unpublished work *Noticias de los arquitectos, arquitectura en España* with his own additions; in volume IV, pages 240 and 305 there are references to Goya. Ceán Bermúdez, who was a close friend of his fellow Asturian Jovellanos, was probably the leading art historian of his time; his *Diccionario de los más ilustres profesores de las Bellas Artes en España* (Madrid, 1800) is still unequalled in its kind. Goya painted him twice and his wife once. Ceán Bermúdez is the author of a critical study of Goya's painting of SS. Justa and Rufina for the Cathedral of Seville (*Análisis de un cuadro que pintó Don Francisco de Goya para la Catedral de Sevilla*, Seville, 1817). The architects Ventura Rodríguez (1717-1785) and Juan de Villanueva (1739-1811) together represent the development of Spanish architecture in Goya's time and both were portrayed by him. Finally, Isidoro Maíquez (1768-1820) was a famous actor from Cartagena whose popularity stemmed from his natural manner of acting; Goya's portrait of Maíquez can be found in the Prado. He took an active part in the uprising on May 2nd 1808 and died in Granada.

72

así estoy

grandson Mariano. His relations with Leocadia Weiss (née Zorrilla) in his ripe old age were most probably not virtuous and towards the end even stormy, but against that background at Bordeaux the figure of a little girl stands out: Rosarito, the daughter of Leocadia (and Goya?...).

With his family and close friends Goya was good-humoured, as can be seen in one of his letters to Zapater (whom he usually addresses as "Dear Martín" or "My dear boy"),

Caricatured self-portrait. This surprising drawing appears in one of Goya's most famous letters to Martín Zapater (jokingly dated in 1800 in London), in which he refers to the Duchess of Alba. It is a vigorous caricature of Goya seated, with an outsize head in profile and the words "This is the way I am" coming out of his mouth. Most of the letter strikes a carefree tone: this light-hearted sketch is significant in a letter probably written soon after suffering the serious illness that deprived him of his hearing.

in which he remarks that he had not given a certain sum of money to a correspondent saying "I don't know why. Nor do I know why we don't write, nor why you are you and I am I, nor why you don't enjoy yourself and I don't either, nor why we live so far apart; nor why you don't marry and are such a rascal, nor why I am so fond of you either, your Paco" (Paco = familiar form of Francisco). Along with this letter we could refer to many others containing unprintable expressions that we will therefore refrain from quoting here.

Goya's letters to Zapater reflect his concern for material affairs. They include constant references to financial matters that reveal how important a well-lined purse was to Goya. This is made evident by his frequent changes of horses and carriages. In connection with these material preoccupations the continual worries caused by his relatives cannot be overlooked. Not only did he help his parents economically, but also his brothers and sister in Saragossa. He went to great trouble to find employment for his brother Camilo (who ended up as a chaplain in Chinchón, near Madrid). His other brother and sister were still more of a burden and among his references to Tomás and Rita, he mentions in his letters how he had to help the latter financially in 1787, 1789 and 1790. It is easy

Self-portrait. Prado, Madrid. After the Peninsular War was over Goya resumed his activity as a portraitist with two self-portraits, one in the Prado and the other in the Academy of San Fernando in Madrid. They complement one another and offer us the serious face of an artist about to turn seventy. Here he disregards dress and concentrates on the expression of his eyes and a mood that breathes pessimism.

to imagine how tiresome it was for Goya to have to respond to his relatives' constant requests for support[37].

Goya appreciated a well-supplied table and his correspondence contains frequent references to different varieties of sausages and sweetmeats that he regularly received from Saragossa, especially at

---

37. For background information about Goya's family, the works by Lafuente Ferrari (1947, page 286), the Marquis of Saltillo (1952) and Salas (1977) should be consulted, as well as his letters to Martín Zapater edited by Mercedes Agueda and Salas (1982); the notes include interesting facts about Camilo Goya (who was baptized in Saragossa in 1753 and died in Chinchón, near Madrid, on September 13th 1828, several months after his brother's death), Tomás (who was born in 1738 and became a gilder like his father) and the unfortunate Rita (born in 1737), who lived with her mother at the artist's expense after their father died on December 17th 1781.

Christmas. He is particularly eloquent when he comments on the arrival of the typical Christmas sweet called *"turrón"*. He also often mentions the thick chocolate drink which used to be the traditional breakfast beverage in Spain.

Much could be written about Goya's love of hunting. His letters are full of mentions of this sport and often enumerate the animals and birds shot on specific days. He was particularly pleased and even proud to have accompanied the Infante Don Luis shooting on two occasions during his stay at Arenas de San Pedro. His fondness for dogs is also registered in his correspondence during 1785 and 1786.

His interest in the so-called *"fiesta nacional"*, the bullfight, is sufficiently well-known since it is upheld both by historical facts and other uncertified sources: legend has it that he arrived in Italy accompanied by a group of bullfighters. Since we are only dealing with documented facts here, we must point out that the first reference to this subject dates from a 1778 letter in which he jokes about the two top bullfighters of the day, Romero and Costillares[38]. In addition to written references we also have all his painted and etched versions of bullfight scenes.

If we want to consider Goya as a painter of religious pictures we should take note of his devotion to the patroness of Saragossa, the Virgin of the Pillar. But we should not overlook the fact that a large number of his drawings and engravings vouch for his anticlerical feelings. It is a point that does not need to be stressed.

38. Pedro Romero (1754-1839) was a famous bullfighter from Ronda who triumphed in Madrid from 1775 on. He retired to Ronda at the age of 45, but was called to Seville in 1830 by Ferdinand VII to be appointed head of the School of Tauromachy. Pedro Joaquín Rodríguez, known as "Costillares" (1746-1800), created the so-called Sevillian manner of bullfighting. He began to make a name for himself in Madrid in 1767 and became Pedro Romero's eternal rival. Two portraits of Costillares by Goya are known.

THE PAINTINGS

After this brief look at his life, we are in a better position to approach Goya's artistic production, which reveals his genius in the most conclusive terms. An overwhelming number of paintings, drawings and etchings are sufficient proof of his exceptional position in the history of art, which is justified not only by the great variety of his own works, but also by his influence on the aesthetic ideas of his age. He was a many-sided painter in that he did not hesitate to try his hand on all those branches of painting that require a large measure of expressiveness. In this respect his major concern was the human interest of whatever he was portraying. This would explain why certain branches of painting are almost totally lacking in his repertory, for example landscapes painted as an end in themselves, out of a sensibility towards nature. He did not follow in Velázquez's steps in this respect, although he did include certain landscapes as backgrounds to his paintings. He has also been considered a poor painter of animals and still-lifes had very little appeal for him.

It is worthwhile to examine Goya's work according to these different branches in order to understand better the artist's mind and follow his stylistic evolution, not only in the changing technique of his brushwork but also in the way he interprets his subjects. It can prove interesting to observe the chronological limits separating each of these branches and draw conclusions, both qualitative and quantitative.

Goya has left us an impressing testimony of his time in his paintings, drawings and etchings, resorting to a different kind of artistic language in each case. On some occasions he complied with the rules laid down by the Academy, portraying a conventional world where all is order and decorum, whereas other works reflect strong opposition to these same patterns of well-bred society. His works are nearly always extraordinarily revealing as records of

Details of Aquelarre *and* The Family of Charles IV. *Prado, Madrid. It is a revealing experience to observe the development of Goya's brushwork. The different stages could be divided up to fit into the different reigns. Under Charles III Mengs' influence can be felt in Goya's careful technique and precise draughtsmanship with rigorous colour treatment. Later, after Charles III had died (1788), colour became more important, with splashes juxtaposed in an extremely bold manner like in* The Family of Charles IV. *Here we can feel the search for contrasts that was later to be developed by the French Impressionists. A growing use of impasto can be observed, that heralds the replacement of the brush by the spatula. The "Black Paintings", originally murals, are the best examples of the outcome of this development. In these paintings design is overridden by the force of the pictorial subject matter. It is known that these murals were originally only landscapes and that the figures were added later. Goya's expressionistic interpretation of the forms is a foretaste of one of the most important trends in contemporary art.*

his time. But we should be more concerned with finding Goya's personal artistic experience in them. The curiosity of discovering the "philosopher" in Goya has given way nowadays to the fascinating study of his findings as a painter. Examining his changes in style, which sometimes amount to violent about-turns, enables us to come much closer to his genius. In order to approach this study in an absolutely rigorous manner we would have to follow up each of these changes, discarding the idea of classifying his works first. However, we consider it more revealing in this case to group his works according to their genres since this can lead us to interesting conclusions due to the way in which Goya interrupted his activity coinciding with events in his own life.

Religious Paintings

Everything we have heard from history or legends about Goya leads us to suppose that his religious beliefs were not very firm, although in July 1780 he wrote to Zapater: "I do not need much to furnish my home; I believe that an image of Our Lady of the Pillar, a table, five chairs, a frying-pan, a wine-bag, a small guitar, a roasting spit and a can-

The Visitation *and detail of* The Adoration of the Magi. *Aula Dei monastery, Saragossa. The works done by Goya in and around Saragossa after his return from Italy in 1771 display some surprising contrasts in fresco techniques. On the ceiling of the Basilica his figures seem to float amid clouds. However on the walls of the Aula Dei church a more sober and monumental tone prevails. This led some art historians to believe that these frescoes belong to a later period in Goya's development. However that may be, these paintings are important among his religious works.*

dlestick are sufficient". Among the people of Aragón, the devotion for their patron Virgin is taken for granted and Goya must have painted her since he was a child. Sánchez Cantón considered that "Goya was not an unbeliever, nor was he over pious" and that "under the influence of his intellectual friends he sympathized with Encyclopedist ideas and was opposed to monks and the Inquisition". Lafuente Ferrari, for his part, observed that the religious element in Goya "is rendered with difficulties and rebelliousness"; he considered Goya's religious paintings, due in many cases

to the necessity of complying with academic norms, "for the most part clumsy and lacking in expressiveness, revealing the laborious effort he had to put into them, not always with satisfactory results, in order to acquit himself of a task for which he obviously felt little inclination". While agreeing with all this, we might add that in judging Goya's attitude towards religious subjects we cannot overlook the circumstances in which he created his religious paintings.

A closer look at his long life will show us that he gradually drifted away from religious issues, which had ceased to interest him at all by the early years of the 19th century. However, the very contradictions of Goya's early work, in the 1760s and 1770s, reflects a hesitant and inexperienced approach and finally his restraints, which reach heights of intensely devout mysticism. Faced with Goya's religious works as a whole, we come up against the most striking contrasts that make a fascinating study.

Goya's early work, in the 1760s and 1770s, reflects a hesitant and inexperienced approach and finally his complete assimilation of academic norms, which he complied with without resistance. He probably started to paint religious pictures in Luzán's workshop before his first visit to Madrid in 1763. Legend has

it that at the age of twelve he painted versions of *The coming of the Virgin of the Pillar, St. Francis of Paul* and *Our Lady of Mount Carmel* on the reliquary doors in the parish church of Fuendetodos. There is no proof behind the story of a later visit to his native village, when he is supposed to have exclaimed: "Don't say that I painted that!".

The paintings at Fuendetodos, presumably dating from before his first visit to Madrid, were lost in 1936, but others listed by Gudiol, executed for the most part in Saragossa, probably date from 1768-1770, before his departure for Italy. Two companion pieces, *The Virgin of the Pillar appearing to St. James*

83

and *The Holy Family*, reveal the influence of his future brother-in-law, Francisco Bayeu, active in Madrid at the time, whose follower Goya declared himself to be during his stay in Italy. In this context we should mention Longhi's claim, in which he is supported by the Marquis of Lozoya, although not by other prominent art critics, that Goya participated in decorating the little cupola over the chancel in the Trinitarian Church in Rome. The Marquis of Lozoya concedes that "it is an unskilfully painted fresco, done too rapidly... with dull colours, possibly due to his inexperience in the technique of fresco-painting...", but he considers these scenes of Abraham and Moses as a prelude to what Goya was going to paint on his return from Italy, between 1771 and 1774 in Aragón.

Following Goya back to Saragossa and its surroundings, where he worked from 1771 to 1774, we will pass over the four pendentives with *Doctors of the Church* that decorate the hermitage in Muel and are repeated in oval frescoes in the parish church of Remolinos, and turn our attention to the fresco for the ceiling of the Basilica of Our Lady of the Pillar in Saragossa; he submitted the preparatory sketch in November after returning from Italy and painted the fresco between January and June 1772. It represents *Angels adoring God* symbolized by His Name in Hebrew in a triangle and is a work full of movement with spatial effects that reveal the influence of Italian paintings.

The murals that Goya painted in the chapel of the Palace of the Count of Sobradiel must have been of considerable importance, but unfortunately they were removed from the walls and transferred to canvas; they are now dispersed. Among the parts that are still in Spain we should mention the com-

The Virgin Queen of Martyrs. *Sketch for one of the ceilings in the Virgen del Pilar basilica, Saragossa. In 1780, after Goya had been appointed a member of the Royal Academy of Arts, he again participated in the decoration of the basilica, on this occasion with a work that was to cause him some trouble. Apparently the artist's interpretation did not meet with the chapter's approval and Francisco Bayeu was called on to pass judgement on his brother-in-law's work. Today we can appreciate the agility in composition and loose handling of this fresco, which is a foretaste of what Goya was going to create years later in San Antonio de la Florida.*

The Immaculate Conception. *Prado, Madrid. The series that Goya painted for the Calatrava College in Salamanca was lost as a result of the Peninsular War. However, a small picture was discovered in the storerooms of the Prado that was probably a preliminary sketch for one of the most important of these canvases. The subject is interpreted in traditional manner, but giving the figure of the Virgin a vigorous, monumental air and underlining the colour contrasts in her tunic and mantle and the sky.*

panion pieces *St. Joseph's dream* (Fine Arts Museum, Saragossa) and *The Burial of Christ* (Lázaro Galdiano Museum, Madrid). They are almost exact copies of works by Simon Vouet, but it is not known whether Goya saw his works in France on his way home from Italy or whether he knew them from engravings or copies. It is so surprising that Goya should have copied the original models to such an extent that Gudiol suspects that the owners of the Palace, Count and Countess of Gabarda, might have set this condition.

But the paintings mentioned so far are all of little interest in comparison to the murals Goya painted in 1774 for the Aula Dei monastery in Saragossa. Thanks to recent restoration work they can now be viewed in excellent conditions. Critics coincide in considering them "the true climax of Goya's youthful period... the best that the artist executed in this genre... in which Baroque manner and classic feeling merge in a well-balanced synthesis" (Gudiol). Art historian Julián Gállego endorsed this view and pointed out "how exactly these paintings were made to suit the place they were intended for. Goya painted them on the spot, taking into account the viewpoint, lighting, spectators' (i.e. the monks') movements and availing to the utmost of the architectonic facilities and even of its difficulties". We will

St. Francis Borgia taking leave of his family. Marquise of Santa Cruz Collection, Madrid. Two preparatory sketches exist for the paintings that Goya did in 1788 for the Cathedral in Valencia. They reveal an extremely loose technique, but at the same time rigorous composition and draughtsmanship. The architectonic elements such as the staircase and backdrop are unprecedented in Goya's paintings until this moment. He has also taken pains to depict costumes of the saint's time.

refrain from going into all the scenes in detail and enumerating their influences, nor will we describe the work carried out by the Buffet brothers who in the past century repainted a number of murals that had been damaged. Among Goya's works, several scenes of the life of the Virgin and Jesus stand out with their monumental character and solidly modelled figures that lack the impression of striving after effect that can be observed in the cupola of the Basilica in Saragossa. In the *Wedding of the Virgin* the figures of the Virgin, St. Joseph and others have something statuesque about them. In *The Circumcision* and *The Presentation in the Temple* the figures are grouped around the Child in an orderly and

87

Cupola of the hermitage of San
Antonio de la Florida. *Madrid. In the
frescoes in San Antonio de la Florida a
new way of interpreting religious
subjects prevails. Here Goya has
depicted the worldly aspect, although
the subject is a miracle: the
resurrection of a man who had been
murdered so that he can testify the
innocence of the saint's father, who
had been accused of killing him. The
story acts as a pretext to depict a wide
landscape crowded with a motley
assembly of figures of all kinds and
ages, from small boys astride the
balustrade to old men portrayed with
the liveliest of brushstrokes. This
fresco signals the birth of
"Impressionist" painting, which
reached a new peak soon after in* The
Family of Charles IV.

The Last Supper. *Holy Grotto church,
Cadiz. These pictures, probably
painted in 1796 and 1797, are a
landmark in Goya's religious
painting. The volume of these
vigorously modelled figures helps to
create the notion of space in each of
the two semi-circular pictures. A
surprising detail is the reclining,
Roman-style pose of the figures,
unusual not only in Goya, but in
painting in general at the time.*

solemn fashion. In *The Epiphany* the standing or kneeling figures of the Magi lead us towards the Holy Family in brilliantly coloured sequences. In these works their monumental character does not seem out of place despite their simple composition. In the Aula Dei monastery Goya gives us a foretaste of vigorous architectonic masses and landscape backgrounds that he was to develop later on.

A large number of works painted by Goya before he reached the age of 30 were included in an exhibition on "The young Goya" in Saragossa in 1986, which showed that religious subjects accounted for the majority of his early artistic production.

Passing over several other paintings and a few references to religious works in his letters, we come to Goya's admission as a member of the Royal Academy of Fine Arts in 1780. His *Christ crucified* which he presented to this institution, now in the Prado, heralds a new period. Here Goya has toned down emotional aspects in order to underline the almost sculptural quality of the figure. It has been correctly remarked that this work resembles one by Mengs at Aranjuez. The same compliance with academic rules can be found in another work, *The Holy Family* (also in the

Prado), which must date from the same year. Lafuente Ferrari described it rather aptly as "an impotent caricature of Mengs' porcelain-like style". It is a fact that both these works show how Goya adapted his style to the current academic trends.

This period ends with further commissions for the Basilica in Saragossa, which were the cause, as we already mentioned, of serious frictions with his brother-in-law when the Chapter insisted on obtaining Francisco Bayeu's approval for Goya's *Virgin Queen of the Martyrs* and the pendentives with the symbols of *Faith, Fortitude, Charity* and *Patience*. He had to make an extraordinary effort to keep his pride in check. However, apart from these personal questions, we must stress the high quality of these works which were seriously damaged in 1981 and subsequently successfully restored so that they are now visible again in all their freshness. Forty years earlier the art critic Ramón Stolz had examined them in detail and pointed out Goya's great ability as a fresco painter. Some differences can be observed between the two preliminary sketches still in existence and the finished paintings, which show how Goya could adapt to the requirements of the semi-circular shape and make the most of the vibrating colours, applying them with masterly brushstrokes. The art critic Federico Torralba regrets that the merits of this cupola have been underestimated and points out similarities in style to the Aula Dei paintings. He correctly affirms that "some of the figures can be reckoned among Goya's most outstanding works". These frescoes in the Virgin of the Pillar basilica have something of a new-style Baroque air about them, a new compositional order, with a spontaneously popular character that comes out in the realistic portrayal of some of the figures.

In the early 1780s Goya's religious paintings reveal a new dimension when we come to regard his works in the San Francisco el Grande church in Madrid. His letters to Zapater reflect in enthusiastic terms his determination to prove his worth in the canvas representing *St. Bernardine of Siena preaching to Alfonso V of Aragón*. In January 1783 Goya sent his friend one of the preliminary sketches with the explanation: "Of course it is very much a rough sketch and the final painting has changes, but it will give you an idea all the same". In a letter to the Count of Floridablanca two years earlier he mentioned the difficulty of this work "because the composition has to be triangular". We now know that the figure of the preacher addressing the crowd was inspired in a tondo of St. Francis

Seizure of Christ. *Prado, Madrid. This is a brilliant preparatory sketch for the large-scale work that Goya painted for the Sacristy of Toledo Cathedral, to be hung near Greco's famous* Expolio (Disrobing of Christ). *Goya probably took the latter work into account when he painted this Biblical scene and paid the same attention to light, portraying the faces in a manner that sometimes borders on caricature. These aspects bring Rembrandt to mind, whose painting had a profound influence, as we know, on Goya. This sketch with its extraordinarily loose handling heralds, even before the outset of the 19th century, a pictorial development that would reach its height in the "Black Paintings".*

Regis preaching painted for the Novitiate Church by Michel-Ange Houasse. Lafuente Ferrari, who published the letter, pointed out that this picture provides evidence of Goya's aesthetic ideas at the time. It contains certain affectations, but the spellbound multitude with its attention riveted open-mouthed on the saint was to be a useful training ground for Goya. Floridablanca was not very satisfied with this nor with other paintings for St. Francis' Church: he remarked that "they are not much to

speak of". But the effort that Goya put into them can be appreciated in his San Antonio de la Florida frescoes fifteen years later.

The loss of the paintings in the Calatrava College in Salamanca has deprived us of the possibility of assessing Goya's work in 1784. Goya owed this commission to his friend the politician Jovellanos and all that remains is a small sketch for the painting of the *Immaculate Conception* which adorned one of the side altars in the church. Although this sketch had been in the Prado since 1891, it has only been identified in recent years. Xavier de Salas described it as a "preparatory sketch executed with great care at a time when Goya was acquiring a position in Madrid and as such a unique item in the Prado collection. Although not a masterpiece, it contains an attractive landscape and beautiful clear colouring".

The religious compositions that Goya executed in Valdemoro, Valladolid and Valencia up till 1788 reveal how his work was becoming more dense. His version of the *Bishop St. Julian* receiving the martyr's palm from the Virgin (Valdemoro) was examined by Salas to compare it with the preliminary sketch in the Prado. It is not an outstanding work, but it is interesting to observe how Goya mastered the challenge of such a narrow composition. The canvases in St. Anne's Convent in Valladolid are noteworthy; Sánchez Cantón quoted Elías Tormo's opinion that they have been "misquoted, misunderstood and misjudged". Since they were exhibited in Madrid in 1961 their fame has grown and they now rank among Goya's finest religious works. They represent *St. Bernard and St. Robert baptizing, The Death of St. Joseph* and *St. Luitgard praying*. All three scenes are portrayed in noble compositions in which Goya probably intended to avoid Baroque exaggerations, but nevertheless added a touch of restrained emotion that exceeds Neoclassical patterns. As on previous occasions, he resorted to other iconographical precedents and this *Death of St. Joseph* can be related to a work on the same subject in the Cathedral of Granada attributed to Carlo Maratta, as Emilio Orozco pointed out. Sánchez Cantón considered these paintings midway between 17th-century and modern art: "free from violent expressiveness, they are equally far removed from Goya's *Christ crucified* with its cool academic restraint as from the rapture of *Christ's Agony in the Garden* painted 37 years later. These pictures in Valladolid, along with those in Valencia, reveal that Goya had reached his well-balanced maturity as a painter of religious subjects".

The works Goya painted for the Cathedral in Valencia represent *St. Francis Borgia taking leave of his family* and *St. Francis Borgia with the impenitent dying man*; there are also excellent preliminary sketches (in a private collection). The composition of the second work, which has been related to a painting by Houasse, is not as pleasing as the farewell scene, which is portrayed "as if it were an intimate event", as Sánchez Cantón observed.

These works for Valencia Cathedral, which were completed in 1788, end the second period and introduce a pause in Goya's production of religious paintings. The third period begins in the last years of the outgoing century and includes a number of outstanding works, starting with the paintings in the Oratory of the church known as the "Holy Grotto" in Cádiz. Their exact date is controversial, but they are generally considered to belong to the 1790s. Without entering into certain discussions concerning Goya's presence in Cádiz, we should point out the extraordinary interest of these semi-circular paintings that represent *The Last Supper, The miracle of the bread and the fishes* and *The parable of the marriage feast*. The composition of the first work, although there are precedents in Poussin, is original. Christ is surrounded by his dis-

ciples who are reclining on the floor in postures that recall a Roman banquet. The figures are very skilfully posed, contrasting the two in the foreground with their backs to the observer, those on the right in the middle distance and those on the left who seem much further removed. Through this the scene appears very spontaneous, with different parts but balanced by the figure of Christ with a halo presiding over the table.

The paintings in Cádiz are like a foretaste, also in form, of Goya's work in the San Antonio de la Florida chapel in 1798. Numerous studies have been made on the subject of these frescoes, but the most conclusive one was published by Skira with Lafuente Ferrari's text and an appendix on technical aspects by the painter Ramón Stolz. This work put an end to all the speculations and doubts about the frescoes. Summing up, Stolz observed: "For the first time Goya paid attention to the joins in the plaster and retouched them, as all fresco painters did, with tempera. He used some bright colours, for example vermilion, on dry plaster and in tempera. He also did it with some shades of blue, but only with loose brushstrokes, never stippling. In the preparatory sketches he followed his usual method: just a few strokes to indicate proportions and general position. Nothing but super-

95

ficial guidelines to help him start painting, no details at all…".

It is unnecessary to dwell on Goya's technique because what really attracts and fascinates the observer here in the cupola and pendentives of San Antonio de la Florida is the essence of painting itself, like an outburst of colour that spills over the figures behind a make-believe balustrade. The angels below the cupola act as "decorative contrasts", as Lafuente Ferrari aptly put it. Although they lose part of their colour values when viewed from a distance, the figures in the crowd are strikingly vigorous as they watch the miracle of St. Anthony bringing a man back to life so that he can exonerate the saint's father, who had been accused of killing him. Goya used bold brushstrokes, often disconnected and juxtaposed, with energetic contrasts, although "he chose black as his base and the greys that emerge when it mixes with the plaster; in this way he produced the effect of masses", as Lafuente Ferrari wrote, following up Stolz's observations. The effects that Goya achieved in San Antonio de la Florida situate these frescoes at the starting-point of Goyesque impressionism. This makes them more important artistically speaking than as a purely religious work; the devotional aspect is a secondary one, although the event it relates is depicted in all its

The Last Communion of St. Joseph of Calasanz. Escuelas Pías de San Antón, Madrid. Goya's evolution as a painter of religious works closes with this canvas painted in 1819. Art historian Salas has pointed out certain similarities between this work and one by Crespi that Goya probably saw in Rome or another one by Ribera that was at El Escorial at the time. However, Goya's own bold brushwork, colour contrasts and light effects stand out in this canvas over , and above such possible influences. Stylistically its handling comes close to that of the "Black Paintings" with which he covered the walls of his country house shortly afterwards. Critics have drawn attention to the emotional aspect of this work which vibrates with a religious feeling not usually found in Goya's painting. Possibly the reason lies in the artist's childhood memories of his own education at a school run by the same religious order for which he was painting this scene, the Scolapians.

supernatural implication, despite the fact that Goya represented it outdoors and not in a courtroom as Father Croisset described it in his "Christian Yearbook".

In this same year (1798) Goya painted other extremely vivid re-

96

ligious works. A *St. Gregory* belonging to a series of *Doctors of the Church* is now in the Romantic Museum in Madrid. Colour seems to be the most important element in this picture too. The Pope is seated, writing in a book, and light falls on his tiara and robes producing beautiful golden reflections. This work is far removed from those Goya painted fifteen years earlier.

This period closes with a surprising work: *The Seizure of Christ* in the Cathedral sacristy in Toledo. Christ's head is surrounded by a number of gesticulating, distorted faces that were subsequently to become characteristic of Goya's art. Some critics have discovered the influence of Rembrandt in this work. The light illuminating it from the left has that strange, unreal quality that can be found in the Dutch master's works. It should also be borne in mind that this picture was intended to be hung next to Greco's famous *Expolio (Disrobing of Christ)*. It is easy to imagine that Goya took this into account. In both works the serene expression on Christ's face contrasts with those of the surrounding figures. It is a stimulating experience to be able to view the two works close together in the sacristy of Toledo Cathedral.

The last period of Goya's religious paintings comprises the years 1812-1819, because we have to pass over another interval of fourteen years to reach his next religious subject, *The Assumption of the Virgin*, painted for the village church of Chinchón during the Peninsular War. His brother Camilo had been a priest there since 1784, thanks to the Infante Don Luis' patronage, and Goya probably painted it for this reason, although not over-enthusiastically. The figure of the Virgin seems somewhat artificial, but the angels in the lower part are excellent.

Five years later, in 1817, Goya painted *St. Justa and St. Rufina* for the Cathedral of Seville, in which he added the words "Caesar Augustus and First Court Painter to the King" to his signature. The king at the time was Ferdinand VII, for whom Goya harboured little sympathy. As Sánchez Cantón commented, this work came into being "as a commission and due to an alien Minerva" and gave rise to very controversial criticism, to the extent that Count de la Viñaza called it "the most profane, worldly and unfortunate of Goya's religious paintings". However, over and beyond all conventional considerations, it is a work that deserves a favourable review: it unquestionably has merits, especially with regard to its colouring. Goya's brushwork technique, loose in his handling of the draperies and other details, connect with his next two works, which bring us to the end of this chapter on his religious paintings.

They date from 1819 and were painted for the schools known as "Escuelas Pías de San Antón" in Madrid. They can rightly be considered outstanding due to their emotional impact. One represents *The Last Communion of St. Joseph Calasanz* and the other *Agony in the Garden*. Both of them repeat a detail already to be found in the above-mentioned work in Seville: a ray of light falling on the principal figures. Goya's brushwork is heavily impasted and his technique increasingly bold, almost like that of a sketch. Some critics believe that a precedent for *The Last Communion* can be found in a work by Crespi, but that should not detract from the emotional value of Goya's saint. The scene is complemented by a series of figures in the background, who however do not distract the observer's attention from the dramatic foreground where the priest is administering the communion to the dying saint. In *Agony in the Garden* the figures of the angel and Christ with outstretched arms stand out against the dark background in a diagonally shaped composition full of expressive impact and Baroque feeling. At this point Goya's brushwork gives way to the most drastic expressionism, calling Rembrandt to mind once again.

Tapestry cartoons

Goya's work as a designer of cartoons for the Royal Tapestry Manufactory reveals a very attractive side of his personality, although sometimes also a rather contradictory one. Contemplating the collection of cartoons in the Prado we should bear in mind that they were intended as vehicles for designs that would only take shape as finished products when they were transformed into tapestries. They were therefore something like the work of a craftsman. For this reason they were stored for many years and only put on display in 1928 when the first centenary of Goya's death was commemorated.

The literature on the subject of these tapestry cartoons is not very abundant for the same reason. In the last century Cruzada Villaamil's study can be highlighted and in the present century Valentín de Sambricio published a very detailed work coinciding with the 200th anniversary of the artist's birth. From this study we know that Goya worked for the Royal Tapestry Manufactory, which Philip V had founded in 1720, for eighteen years, starting in 1775, although nominally he belonged to the staff until 1800. For almost twenty years therefore he submitted designs at irregular intervals, sometimes working intensively and extremely   99 rapidly and at other times letting periods of over five years pass by without preparing a design. In 1775, for example, he painted nine cartoons, the following year only one; in 1777 and 1778 there were five each year and during the next two years he submitted eight and eleven designs respectively, followed by an interval of more than five years without producing a single cartoon. In 1786, however, he painted thirteen, none in 1787, three in 1788, one in 1789, none in 1790 and finally seven between 1791 and 1792, making a total of sixty-three, apart from some copies and sketches.

Professor Camón Aznar considered 1793 an all-important year in Goya's artistic activity "when he freed himself from the Royal Tapestry Manufactory's commissions and opened up his imagination to the pure changes of his inspiration. This is the period of his *invented paintings*". This opinion may well indicate one of the various turning-points in Goya's artistic career, but it also marks the end of a period in which he was able to express himself spontaneously and vitally in an important series of paintings on popular, every-day subjects. It is true that the painters who depicted these typical rustic scenes for the Royal Tapestry Manufactory were only continuing a style that had been widely developed in 17th-

Off to the hunt. Prado, Madrid. This belongs to a series of hunting scenes that Goya painted as designs for tapestries to cover the walls of the Prince of Asturias' dining-room at El Escorial. It is dated in 1775 and was not considered to be by Goya until Sambricio identified it. It shows that Goya was not very expert at painting animals, but the nine scenes that made up this series served their purpose as decorations. They are related to the style of his brothers-in-law of the Bayeu family.

century Flemish painting and became a favourite theme for Spanish tapestries from the start. It should be recalled that the initiator of the tapestry manufacture in Spain, Jacob van der Goten, began his work in Madrid making copies after Teniers and Wouwermans on his looms. However, apart from these precedents, Goya's contribution to this so-called *costumbrista* style "consists in producing a new image, a new manner of observing —and imagining— everyday reality", as Valeriano Bozal correctly points out in a work published in 1983.

It is extremely revealing to imagine Goya working along with other painters for the Tapestry Manufac-

100

tory and to make comparisons between their designs as far as subject-matter and quality are concerned. Comparing some of his cartoons with those of equally prestigious painters (like his brother-in-law Ramón Bayeu, for example), the differences may appear enormous; however, we should not overlook the fact that some unquestionably fine cartoons, such as those by José del Castillo, were also produced in the Royal Tapestry Manufactory. For Goya the experience was in the long run enriching, although a tedious one.

Most of Goya's cartoons are kept in the Prado and are highly interesting from a historical point of view. Next to them we should also examine the few drawings and preparatory sketches still in existence that were part of the long tapestry manufacturing process. The architect Sabatini wrote at one point that after the director of the factory had taken the measurements for the tapestries, "now the king must choose the subjects that he wants to be depicted... When His Majesty has decided this, the artists will make preparatory sketches to be submitted to the king... and then the full-size pictures corresponding to the measurements of the tapestries, to be submitted again to His Majesty before being sent to the Manufactory to be made up...". These lines show just how impor-

tant a part the king played in the final decisions concerning the subject-matter of these tapestries, although the artists (and in particular Goya owing to his temperament) had a fairly free hand in the early stages.

Goya's designs were intended for tapestries to adorn the royal chambers at El Escorial and the Pardo Palace. The Bourbon kings wanted to redecorate the private suites used by the Royal family after the 16th-century monastery building at El Escorial had been extended. The cartoons should therefore be visualized in the rooms for which they were painted, but in the form of tapestries; in order to judge them correctly they have to be imagined covering the four walls of each of the rooms they were intended for, that is, as parts of a complete decoration, coordinated in their subject-matter and compositional form. Due to problems of space and other difficulties it has not been possible to reproduce this atmosphere in the Prado Museum and display the cartoons as the tapestries were originally intended to be viewed. Here we will attempt to point out their most important features.

The dining-room used by the Crown Prince and Princess at El Escorial was the first decoration that Goya undertook in 1775. He painted nine cartoons for this room,

all except one *(The angler)* depicting hunting scenes. The largest was *Shooting quail;* others include *Hunting a wild boar, A huntsman loading his gun* and similar subjects. The varying measurements of these cartoons show that they were meant for tapestries to cover the spaces between doors and windows and over these openings. Although Goya was a keen hunter himself, we must admit that these pictures do not yet reveal his genius and in fact the animals are far from ably portrayed.

The same royal couple's dining-room at the Pardo Palace was

The picnic. *Prado, Madrid. This is a tapestry cartoon painted in 1776 for the Prince of Asturias' dining-room at the Pardo Palace. It is one of a series of ten illustrating popular scenes, executed in an experienced manner, some of them large-size. Goya's approach is direct and the figures are made to appear full of life. It is a companion piece to his* Dance on the banks of the River Manzanares *and probably likewise represents a spot near the Casa de Campo park.*

The parasol. *Prado, Madrid. This small canvas is one of a series of cartoons that Goya delivered to the Royal Tapestry Manufactory in 1777. It was intended for a space over a door and with its simple pyramid-shaped composition probably took into account the way light would fall on it from a nearby balcony. Goya may have found inspiration in a painting by Ranc, who worked in Madrid for Philip V, that depicts the myth of Vertumnus and Pomona (now in the Fabre Museum in Montpellier, France).*

The wine-harvest. *Prado, Madrid. This tapestry cartoon belongs to a series of thirteen that Goya painted for Charles III in 1786, that is, two years before the king died. It included four on the Seasons. This one alludes to Autumn. It is one of the most successful of this group with its agile composition and insistence on mass and space: the impression of depth is heightened by the smaller figures in the background.*

Goya's second commission and he carried it out between 1776 and 1778. He was again working for the future Charles IV and his wife María Luisa and this time the scenes are popular ones, interpreted in ten skilful cartoons. To preside over the room he painted the 4-metre long *Quarrel in the New Tavern*. Other subjects include *The maja and the cloaked men, The picnic, The kite, Card-players* and *Dance on the bank of the Manzanares*, which altogether must have made a highly attractive decoration. In the scene with the group dancing on the river bank the dome of San Francisco el Grande can be distinguished in the background. Scenes such as *The drinker, The parasol, Boys picking fruit* and *Children blowing up a balloon*, intended for the spaces over doors and windows, completed the decoration of this dining-room.

This royal couple's bedroom in the Pardo Palace was to be decorated with seven tapestries, for which Goya submitted cartoons between January and July 1779. He again depicted popular Madrid scenes, presided over by a large-scale design of a *Ball game* which with its 4.70 metres must have filled the northern wall, while *The Madrid Fair* and *The pottery vendor*, 2.20 metres long each, must have been intended to cover the eastern and western walls. Several narrower scenes were probably meant for the southern wall, whereas others, portraying children's pastimes, were for spaces over doors. Apart from some compositional problems, the fine quality of some of these designs should be underlined, especially *The pottery vendor*.

The adjoining dressing-room in the Pardo Palace must have worried Goya. Some of the cartoons he presented to the Manufactory between April 1778 and January 1780 were turned down. One of the most popular scenes, *The blind man with a guitar*, had to be withdrawn because it did not comply with the requirements of this room. An engraving exists which reveals that he altered the composition. However, this work (which apparently represents the old Madrid Barley Market or *Plaza de la Cebada*) is one of the most expressive of this group; the rascally look in the eyes of the blind man's guide boy seems to compensate for his master's lack of eyesight. In all Goya made thirteen cartoons for this antechamber, many of them very lively scenes such as *The young bulls* (which possibly contains a self-portrait), *The tobacco guards* with a splendid landscape, *The washerwomen, The swing, The woodcutters, Young man with a guitar* as well as others meant to fill high narrow spaces between doors or low wide ones to place over doors.

The pottery vendor. *Prado, Madrid.*
This tapestry cartoon was a design
to decorate the Prince of Asturias'
bedroom at the Pardo Palace. It dates
from 1779 and belongs to a series of
seven, all depicting popular scenes,
that was continued in a second series
intended for the ante-chamber. Goya

described it as "representing a man
from Valencia selling crockery, two
ladies sitting on the ground
choosing..., an old woman..., two
gentlemen looking at the carriage...".
All this and more, presumably with a
view of Madrid in the background, is
depicted in this colourful scene.

St. Isidore's hermitage. *Prado, Madrid. This is one of the preparatory sketches for tapestries intended to cover the walls of the so-called Princesses' bedroom at the Pardo Palace, but the tapestry was never made from it because Charles III's death prevented this series from being carried out. Only the cartoon of* Blind man's buff *was used. This delightful view of St. Isidore's hermitage was finally sold to the Duke of Osuna in 1799. It would probably have been a companion piece to* Blind man's buff. *The vigorous mass of the church serves as a contrast to the figures in the fore- and background.*

The king's dining-room in the Pardo Palace offered Goya the opportunity of painting a very ambitious series of cartoons. From June 1786 on, that is after an interval of six years and when Ramón Bayeu and Goya were appointed sole designers of the Royal Tapestry Manufactory, Goya produced over a dozen cartoons. The most important were the series on the four seasons, represented by *The flower girls, The threshing-floor, The wine-harvest* and *The snowstorm.* Each of these works deserves recognition for its composition and colouring, including the wintry scene that is kept in whitish tones with little scope for contrasts; this

design was probably planned to occupy a space against the light, between the two balconies, whereas the 6-metre long summer scene *(The threshing-floor)* with its golden tones was meant for the wall opposite. Two narrow pictures, *Poor children at the well* and *The injured mason*, seem rather disconcerting if we consider them as reflections on social affairs. However, the original sketch for the latter depicted a drunken labourer rather than an accident at work. Maybe Goya's first idea was to contrast allegories of wine and water. Certainly the great dining-room at the Pardo Palace had a highly interesting decorative scheme with these

St. Isidore's Meadow. *Prado, Madrid. This masterly sketch for a tapestry cartoon that was never carried out makes it easy to imagine what a magnificent work the final design would have been, knowing that the required measurements were 7.56 × 3.5 metres. Goya's desire to make a success of this composition can be seen in a letter to his friend Martin Zapater dated May 31st 1788, where he expresses his concern "because time is short and it is something that the king, the Crown Prince and Princess, etc. have to see, as well as being a difficult subject and one that needs a lot of work since it shows St. Isidore's Meadow on the saint's feast-day with all the bustle there is in this city on such an occasion".*

109

tapestry designs and other smaller ones over the doors and windows.

One of these small-size compositions showed *Two cats fighting*; it was discovered among the many works stored in the Prado deposit room and identified by Mercedes Agueda in 1984; it is now on display in the gallery rooms.

The Princesses' bedroom was the final project that Goya worked on for the palace at El Pardo. The documents on this period are incomplete, so it is extremely difficult to clear up any doubts about it. We should now speak more of preparatory sketches than of actual tapestry cartoons; one of these is of exceptional quality: *St. Isidore's Meadow*. In a letter to his friend Zapater dated May 31st 1788, Goya wrote that he was "working very hard and with certain anxiety because there is little time and it is something that the King, Prince and Princess and others have to see; in addition the subject is difficult and requires so much work because it shows St. Isidore's Meadow on the saint's feast-day, with all the bustle that is usual here in this city...". And Goya added: "I can assure you as my friend that I have my doubts about it and my mind will not be at rest until this matter has been accomplished; this is no life...". Goya's words are significant enough; unfortunately the sketch was not converted into a cartoon, but we know

from the frame that the tapestry was intended to measure 7.56 metres in width by 3.50 metres in height. Let us try to imagine it accompanied by *Blind man's buff* and *St. Isidore's hermitage*... The death of Charles III probably prevented this splendid series of tapestries from being carried out. The small-scale sketch of *St. Isidore's Meadow* is the most beautiful landscape that Goya painted and includes a view of Madrid across the river as it was until speculators destroyed the pleasant scenery of the Manzanares valley in recent times. The painting recalls Velázquez's *View of Saragossa*, with which Goya, as a good Aragonese, must have been very familiar.

During 1791 and 1792 Goya produced seven tapestry cartoons for the king's study at El Escorial monastery. We know that thirteen had been ordered and with the evidence at hand it is difficult to make conjectures about whether the missing cartoons were carried out or not. These seven include such popular scenes as *The stilts*, *Young girls with pitchers*, *The straw manikin* and especially *The wedding*, which to judge by its measurements was intended to preside over the king's study. It represents the marriage of a pretty young girl to an ungainly old man and anticipates the "invented" subject-matter full of satirical meaning that Goya was to paint

after the serious illness that caused his permanent deafness. The sarcastic expression of the priest and the children's mocking attitudes are a foretaste of the genre scenes that Goya produced at the end of the 18th and beginning of the 19th century.

It is evident that during these last years of his activity for the Royal Tapestry Manufactory Goya was increasingly unwilling to carry out the commissioned works. He probably found it frustrating to paint these tapestry cartoons whose sole object was to serve as models for the weavers to reproduce the artist's

Blind man's buff. *Prado, Madrid. In 1788, the year Charles III died, Goya made four preparatory sketches for cartoons meant for tapestries to decorate the Princesses' bedroom at the Pardo Palace. This is the only one that reached the stage of a cartoon for the Royal Tapestry Manufactury. The subject of this popular game offered Goya the opportunity of depicting a variety of poses. The faces of the female figures on the sides are rather expressionless.*

The stilts. The straw manikin. *Prado, Madrid. The last tapestry cartoons designed by Goya were those he painted in 1791 and 1792 for the king's study at El Escorial. He only finished seven of the thirteen designs originally intended for this room, but three of them are really outstanding works, first and foremost* The wedding *and then the two reproduced here. This series can be considered the brilliant end of a period in his artistic production, shortly before he contracted the serious illness that was going to be the cause of his deafness. His activity as a tapestry designer ends in El Escorial where it had begun in 1775. These two cartoons reflect an optimistic aspect of Goya's work, depicting gay pastimes and scenes of everyday life in a vivid, juicy manner.*

juicy colours with woollen threads in an unfair competition. Unfortunately Goya did not live to see how an important part of his work has been recovered and rehabilitated in the 20th century.

Portraits

When we reviewed Goya's life we already stressed the influence that the world around him had on his personality. He was a witness to crucial events in Spanish history and as a painter left us an invaluable series of portraits depicting some of the key figures of his time. No other artist in Spain can be said to have done so much in this respect, not even Velázquez or Greco who were both outstanding portraitists. Possibly Goya's portraits do not reach the high standard of these two masters' works, but they contain the most real, human and penetrating image of the personalities that he knew during his long life. Moreover, there are practically no interruptions in his activity as a portrait painter. However, this does not imply an equally high standard of quality in all his portraits, as we have indicated. Some seem to have been executed merely as a routine, out of the artist's need to earn his living, whereas others are masterly and reveal Goya's generous, enthusiastic intention of capturing his sitter's whole spirit.

Goya's enormous output of portraits covers 57 years of his life. If we leave out those that are difficult to date due to lack of documental proof and taking into account only the most notable and correctly dated works, we can follow Goya's development as a portraitist, observing how his brushwork became more incisive, rapid and vibrating as he disclosed his sitter's psychological characteristics. This is accompanied by a gradual evolution in his colouring, beginning with pearly tints in his early works and ending with heavily impasted dark tones in his Bordeaux portraits. These paintings can also be subdivided, regardless of their chronological order, into various groups. For example, his treatment of children, irrespective of their social condition, is always particularly tender. On the other hand, a bitingly ironical attitude comes to the fore in many of his courtly portraits, especially in *The Family of Charles IV*. A feeling for refined elegance is evident in portraits of personalities like the *Count of Fernán Núñez*[39], whereas affection, if not

39. Carlos José Gutiérrez de los Ríos, 7th Count of Fernán Núñez, was born in Lisbon in 1779 and died, apparently after being thrown by a horse, in 1822. He was Spanish ambassador to London and Lisbon and also attended the Congress of Vienna in his diplomatic capacity. Ferdinand VII granted him the title of Duke in 1817.

114

outright compassion, can be sensed in the image of Godoy's unfortunate wife, the *Countess of Chinchón*.

The first known portrait by Goya was painted in Italy when he was 25. It represents *Don Manuel de Vargas Machuca*[40] and is now in

Self-portrait (?) Museo de Bellas Artes, Saragossa. Goya portrayed himself at regular intervals from his youth until his old age, as is well-known. This fine study of a young man's head under a wide-brimmed hat might be one of the first in his series of self-portraits.

40. The only identification of the sitter is to be found on a slip of paper stuck to the back of this portrait. The Marquis of Lozoya (1956, page 64), "overcoming his instinctive mistrust of such testimonies", investigated the history of the Aragonese family Vargas Machuca that settled in Italy in the 17th century but found no Manuel. However, there is evidence of the presence in Naples of the 3rd Duke of Vargas

Sao Paulo (Brasil). Commenting on it the Marquis of Lozoya referred to its "discreet handling and not particularly high quality". It is painted according to the rules laid down by Mengs; composition and facial traits conform to what can be called the style of the period and there are no clear-cut features that could individualize the sitter. Much the same can be said about his portrait of the *Count of Miranda*[41] (Lázaro Galdiano Museum, Madrid), dated 1774, which belongs to Goya's first period in Madrid, a year after his marriage to Josefa Bayeu. He also painted two self-portraits (Zurgena Collection, Madrid and Museum of Saragossa) around this time, which brings us to a subdivision in his portraiture; Julián Gállego made a study of this aspect of the artist's production, which seems to have been one of his favourites. None of these portraits is of particular artistic value, but they are interesting as

a foretaste of what Goya would be capable of doing in the 1780s.

After being admitted to the Academy and overcoming the friction caused by his sketches for the Basilica in Saragossa, Goya embarked on several different activities. Leaving aside a few minor portraits, we should turn to the works he executed for the Infante Don Luis. Goya's stay at his palace in Arenas de San Pedro in 1783 was particularly fruitful. He painted the heads in profile of the Infante and his wife (as mentioned, he had contracted a morganatic marriage with María Teresa Vallabriga), as if he were making first sketches for the three-quarter portraits (Munich and Cleveland Museums) that he painted later in a somewhat courtly style. He then portrayed the children full-length: Luis María, who was 6 years and 3 months old at the time and was later to become Archbishop of Toledo, and María Teresa at the age of two years and nine months, who in time was to marry Godoy. This very attractive portrait, now in the National Gallery in Washington, depicts the little girl with a dog against a landscape that resembles the Gredos Mountains (behind the small town of Arenas de San Pedro). The portrait of her mother *María Teresa Vallabriga on horseback* also has mountains in the background and seems a forerunner of Goya's future

Machuca, whose name was Miguel and who lived from 1733 to 1795; so probably this is a case of a mistaken Christian name.

41. His name was Pedro Alcántara, 14th Duke of Zúñiga as well as 10th Duke of Peñaranda (1741-1790). Some experts do not agree about attributing this work to Goya. Gudiol (1970, page 242) includes it in his Catalogue "with certain reservations". Sánchez Cantón (1951, page 20, plate VI) quoted the correct date in his text, although that of 1777 appears in the plate; he remarked that the work is "far from perfect".

The Family of Charles IV. *Prado, Madrid. In a letter to Godoy dated April 22nd 1800 in Aranjuez the Queen wrote: "The King says that when Goya has finished the portrait of your wife (i.e. the famous portrait of the* Countess of Chinchón) *he should come here to paint all of us together".*

In order to capture the likeness of each of the members of the family Goya made a series of studies of the different heads. The painting was completed by June of the following year. It is his masterpiece and probably the last important work he carried out as Painter to the King.

117

large-scale paintings of the king and queen; he might possibly have had in mind Velázquez's version of Queen Isabel of Bourbon, the wife of Philip IV. All these paintings, important as they were, cannot compare with *The Family of the Infante Don Luis*, whose existence was known thanks to a mention by Gudiol and which was then "rediscovered" in Italy, where it was examined in detail by Gassier. There is a reduced version of this large-scale work in the collection of the Duke and Duchess of Sueca. The art critic Angulo pointed out the bourgeois atmosphere of this group portrait, which does not seem to be the family of the king's younger brother, but rather that of his wife, a commoner. From a sociological point of view, this portrait has no precedents in Spanish art, although there is a remote similarity with Velázquez's *"Las Meninas"* (or *The Maids of Honour*) in that Goya portrayed himself working on the painting. The precedents of this composition cannot be traced in the history of Spanish art. Gassier studied this work in 1979 from a pictorial point of view and underlined the fine quality of its colouring that enhances its composition. It contains a number of standing figures and only the Infante and his wife are seated at a table. It is revealing that she is portrayed having her hair dressed, thus stressing the homely atmosphere of this family portrait.

The architect Ventura Rodríguez. Nationalmuseum, Stockholm. The inscription in the picture contains precise information: "Original portrait of Don Ventura Rodríguez, architect to His Serene Highness Infante Don Luis and chief master of the City of Madrid, painted by order of His Highness' Illustrious wife, by Don Francisco Goya in the year 1784". The canvas is therefore associated with the world of the ill-fated Infante Don Luis in Arenas de San Pedro. The plan that the architect is holding in the portrait is that of the Lady chapel in the basilica of Our Lady of the Pillar in Saragossa.

A woman combing her hair is also the subject-matter of a sketch by Goya, that could well be related to this painting. Valentín de Sambricio pointed out that the painter Paret had worked for the Infante until 1780; he might well have devised this theme, that was later enlarged upon by Goya.

In 1783 Goya painted another work into which he put all his enthusiasm and best intentions, although the result was not a masterpiece. This was a full-length portrait of José Moñino, *The Count of Floridablanca*, painted full-face with a figure behind him (possibly the architect

119

Sabatini) and on the left side Goya in profile showing him a painting. In addition, on the wall in the background there is an oval portrait of Charles III and on the table a clock and papers, while other papers and a book are lying on the floor. It is understandable that the famous minister was not very satisfied with this portrait overloaded with contrived effects.

From 1783 on there was a steady increase in the list of Goya's sitters, although many of the portraits were merely commissions that contributed towards improving Goya's financial position, so that we can refrain from quoting them all. In the family sphere, he painted a magnificent portrait of his brother-in-law *Francisco Bayeu* (1786), now in the Academy at Valencia, which seems to indicate the end of the friction that had cropped up between the two when Goya was working on the frescoes in Saragossa five years earlier. The three-quarter length portrait of the architect *Ventura Rodríguez* (National Museum, Stockholm), who was working for the Infante Don Luis at the time (1784), is also a fine work. Following along these lines we find a whole series of portraits of personalities who were friends of Goya, like the lawyer and politician *Jovellanos* and the art historian *Ceán Bermúdez* (1784-85). Around the same time Goya painted two more

The Marquise of Pontejos. National Gallery, Washington. Mariana de Pontejos y Saldoval was the wife of the Count of Floridablanca's elder brother; she was widowed and remarried twice. This portrait was painted to mark her first marriage in 1786. It is the first of a series of excellent full-length portraits of female sitters against landscape backgrounds, painted with special attention to textile qualities and elegant poses.

self-portraits, now in the museums of Agen and Castres (France). This was an activity that he kept up all his life, not only in painting, but also in drawings and sometimes caricatures in his letters.

Passing over other examples of his ever-growing activity as a portraitist, we can single out the portrait he painted in 1786 for the San Carlos Bank (now kept in the Bank of Spain) of *Charles III* dressed in hunting attire with a shotgun and a dog, in a Velázquez-inspired composition. There are various versions of this work (in the Prado, Madrid City Hall, Duke of Fernán Núñez's collection and Banco Exterior de

121

España), which seems to indicate that Goya was satisfied with the result.

After *The Family of the Infante Don Luis* Goya undertook another family portrait which is one of his finest group studies, *The Duke and Duchess of Osuna with their children*[42] (Prado, Madrid). This canvas is the best fruit of Goya's relationship with the house of Osuna. He painted the figures with great care, positioning them in a somewhat conventional manner. But the presence of the four children (three standing and the fourth seated on a cushion on the floor) lends the picture a gay, tender air. With them Goya engaged in a branch of portraiture of which he produced numerous examples during his lifetime, always painted with an extremely delicate touch. Around the same time he executed the charming portrait of little *Manuel Osorio*, one of

Josefa Bayeu, Goya's wife. Prado, Madrid. The sitter has generally been identified, although without documental evidence, as Goya's wife. The painting dates from 1798. Josefa Bayeu was born on May 19th 1747, the daughter of Ramón Bayeu and his wife María and sister to the painters Francisco (who protected the family and also Goya in his beginnings), Ramón and Manuel (who became a Carthusian monk). She married Goya in 1773. There are many references to her and her frequent miscarriages in Goya's letters to Martín Zapater. She died in 1812.

the sons of the Count of Altamira, playing with a bird on a string[43]. Another fine example is *Luis María de Cistue*[44] (Frick Collection, New York). Goya usually took great pains over his child portraits and worked at them with a careful, unhurried technique.

---

42. This work is documented in 1788. With reference to the Duke of Osuna, see note 18. The Catalogue of the Prado includes brief biographies of the Duke and Duchess and their children: Francisco de Borja (1785-1820), who inherited the title and sat again for Goya in 1816; Pedro de Alcántara (1786-1851), later Prince of Anglada, who became Director of the Prado and of the Fine Arts Academy of San Fernando; Josefa Manuela (1783-1838), who was painted again by Goya in 1816, and Joaquina (1784-1851), who became the Marquise of Santa Cruz in 1802 and posed for Goya again in a famous painting that has recently been acquired by the Prado.

43. This canvas is in the Metropolitan Museum, New York, and bears an abbreviated inscription: "Don Manuel Osorio Manrique de Zúñiga, Lord of Ginés. Born in April 1784."

44. This portrait bears an inscription: "Don Luis María de Cistué y Martínez at the age of two years and eight months." Since the child was born on July 23rd 1788, the painting can be correctly dated.

123

Approaching the end of the century it steadily becomes more difficult to single out a representative few of Goya's portraits because the evolution of his brushwork is continuous, enabling him to produce works with increasingly bolder colouring. With regard to their technique, his portraits of his brother-in-law *Francisco Bayeu* are noteworthy. The one dated 1795 was exhibited in an unfinished state when Bayeu died that same year; its grey tones are admirable. In the half-length portrait of his wife, *Josefa Bayeu*, and the full-length ones of the *Marquise of Pontejos* (National Gallery, Washington), the *Marquise of Santa Cruz* (Louvre, Paris) and the actress María del Rosario Fernández, called *"La Tirana"* (San Fernando Academy, Madrid), the remarkably fine handling of the draperies catches the eye[45].

Bernardo de Iriarte. *Musée des Beaux Arts, Strasbourg. Deciphering the abbreviations, the inscription reads: "Don Bernardo Iriarte, Vice-Protector of the Royal Academy of the three Noble Arts, portrayed by Goya as a testimony of mutual esteem and affection in the year 1797". He belonged to a well-known family from the Canary Isles; born in Santa Cruz, Tenerife, in 1735, he held posts in Parma and London. He was head of the Academy between 1792 and 1803 and minister under Charles IV and Joseph Bonaparte. He went into exile in Bordeaux and died in 1814.*

---

45. The three full-length female portraits are extremely interesting. The Marquise of Pontejos was María Ana de Pontejos, born about 1763 and married in 1786 to Col. Francisco Moñino, the elder brother of the Count of Floridablanca; the portrait might have been painted for her wedding. When her first husband died the Marquise married Fernando de Silva y Meneses and after she had been widowed again, in 1817 married a much younger man, Joaquín Pérez Vizcaíno y Moles, who lived to be the founder of a famous charitable institution, the Monte de Piedad de Madrid. The Marquise of Santa Cruz portrayed in the painting in the Louvre is not the daughter of the 9th Duke of Osuna, whose portrait Goya also painted, but an attractive lady called Maria Waldstein, who was born in Vienna in 1763 and married the 9th Marquis of Santa Cruz in 1781. She was identified by Jeannine Baticle (1977) and the portrait probably dates from about 1800. Finally, María del Rosario Fernández, known in theatrical circles as "La Tirana", was one of the most famous actresses of Goya's time; he painted at least two portraits of her (one is in the Academy of San Fernando, the other belongs to the March Collection, Madrid).

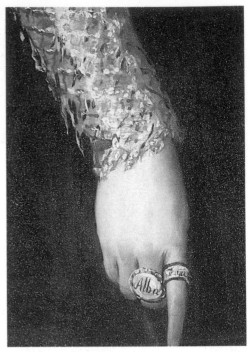

The 13th Duchess of Alba. *Hispanic Society of America, New York. This fine portrait is a significant testimony of Goya's stay in the Coto de Doñana in 1797. When Cayetana's husband died in July 1796 she is known to have retired to Sanlúcar de Barrameda and her magnificent estate on the other side of the Guadalquivir river. Goya joined her there and the ensuing romance was probably only short-lived, contrary to popular legends. Goya portrayed the Duchess in several preparatory drawings, some small paintings and in this full-length picture. He has added a revealing touch in the two rings she is wearing here, inscribed "Alba" and "Goya", and also in the words "Sólo Goya" (Only Goya) written in the sand at her feet.*

Don José Alvárez de Toledo, Marquis of Villafranca and Duke-consort of Alba. *Prado, Madrid. This was probably the first full-length portrait that Goya painted for the house of Alba, to judge by a famous letter dating from 1794 or 1795. The Duke, leaning against a piano, is holding a music notebook entitled "Four songs with pianoforte accompaniment by Mr. Haydn". The Duke was well-known as a music-lover and his tastes probably differed widely from those of his wife Cayetana. He was born on July 16th 1756 and died a week before turning forty.*

Thus we come to the two portraits of the *Duchess of Alba*, dated 1795 and 1796. The first one, dedicated to her on the lower left and kept in the Alba family home, the Liria Palace in Madrid, has an irresistible charm about it, although the figure is slightly stiff. Again Goya's skill comes to the fore in the handling of the draperies, landscape and the little long-haired dog at the Duchess' feet. Although her expression is somewhat lofty, the portrait reproduces faithfully her features with the thick eyebrows and tight lips. A touch of humour is not missing either: the red bows on the Duchess' bodice and in her hair match the one tied round the little dog's hind leg.

The portrait belonging to the Hispanic Society in New York repeats a detail of the one in Madrid: in both the Duchess is pointing to the words that indicate Goya's affection for her. The Madrid portrait, as we have mentioned, includes a simple dedicatory inscription, while the New York one, painted during Goya's stay in Sanlúcar de Barrameda, with its enigmatic words "Only Goya", conjures up visions of the artist putting all his passion into the work. However, nothing but impassivity is to be found in her face, while the artist reveals his mastery in the dark tones of her mantilla and dress. Since it was

The Duchess of Alba and her duenna. Prado, Madrid. This little work has recently been acquired by the Prado. It reflects a gay moment during the artist's stay at the Coto de Doñana, a demostration of Cayetana de Alba's playful mood. Pictorially it is also a masterly work.

cleaned several years ago the work's fine quality can be appreciated again.

In the closing years of the century Goya painted several other excellent portraits, including the *Bullfighter Costillares* (Lázaro Galdiano Museum, Madrid), *Jovellanos,* the *Architect Villanueva* (San Fernando Academy, Madrid), etc. But turning our attention to Goya's activity as a Court Painter, we should consider a number of portraits that are interesting not only for their artistic quality, but also for their historical value. During 1799 and 1800 Goya was occupied in painting portraits of King Charles IV and Queen María Luisa standing and on horseback. These reflect his intention of reproducing a lifelike image

even if the result was not always flattering for his sitters. In both of his portraits the king is wearing the uniform of Colonel of the Guard with the Golden Fleece and the Orders of Charles III and St. Genarus. In her standing portrait the Queen is dressed in black with a mantilla and in the equestrian one she also wears the Guardsman's uniform and is mounted astride her horse. The king's face reveals plainness and simplicity, while the Queen is portrayed without any attempt at concealing her unattractiveness...

However, these individual portraits are outdone by the exceptional *Family of Charles IV*, painted in Aranjuez in the spring of 1800. After excellent restoration work has preserved the painting and revealed its extraordinarily rich colouring, its true worth can now be appreciated. The canvas has gained in depth since a number of details and shades have come to light that were hitherto unknown. This work shows Goya at the height of this artistic career. It is also a counterpart to Velázquez's great work *(Las Meninas)* and similarly has a revealing intention.

In *The Family of Charles IV* the members of the royal family are grouped more or less in a row around the centrally placed figure of Queen María Luisa. From left to right we can identify: Carlos María

Portrait of the Court embroiderer Juan López de Robredo. *Private collection, Madrid. For a long time the sitter was believed to have been Antonio Gasparini, who was a stucco decorator at Court. However, thanks to Luisa Barreno Sevillano's investigations, he has now been identified as a member of a family of embroiderers who worked for the Court and were granted the rank of hidalgos (gentlemen) together with the right to wear embroidered uniforms in 1798. Goya's portrait probably commemorates that event and was therefore presumably painted around that year.*

Isidro (who was later the pretender to the throne when his brother Ferdinand VII died without leaving a male heir); the Prince of Asturias and future Ferdinand VII, who is closest to the viewer; the king's sister María Josefa, who died the following year; an unidentified figure with her face turned away, who possibly represents the future, as yet unknown, bride of Ferdinand VII; next to the Queen is her daughter María Isabel, who married in December 1802 at the age of thirteen. The Queen is holding her

youngest son Francisco de Paula by the hand. Then comes the King and behind him his brother Antonio can be seen as well as his eldest daughter Carlota Joaquina in profile; finally we have the Prince and Princess of Parma or King and Queen of Etruria, Luis of Bourbon and María Luisa (daughter of Charles IV) with her baby son Carlos Luis in her arms. This royal portrait gallery is rounded off with Goya's own self-portrait in the background or in fact two self-portraits if we count the second head that came to light when the picture was restored.

Although the figures are somewhat stiffly posed, with distant and absent-minded expressions on their faces so that the warm cordiality of Velázquez's *Meninas* is missing, it cannot be denied that they are very skilfully positioned, on different planes and yet connected in a masterly manner. Without any strict pattern the figures on the left form a compact group around the future Ferdinand VII. The King and Queen with their youngest children are spaced along a slightly oblique line, while the remaining figures group together on the diagonal in the middle distance with their masses forming a contrast to the King. The two paintings that cover the rear wall have gained considerably from the restoration and now add a further touch of colour, fur-

Portrait of Asensio Juliá (?). Thyssen-Bornemisza Collection, Madrid. This small work is a masterpiece. It is signed "Goya to his friend Asensi" and has given rise to certain doubts about the sitter's identity. It could represent the painter from Valencia Asensio Juliá, known as "El Pescadoret", who helped Goya in San Antonio de la Florida. But in one of Goya's letters to Zapater dating from 1789 there is another reference: "Today Asensio turned up and hopes to pass the test as a master builder at the Academy here".

nishing a fitting counterpart to the richly coloured garments of the main figures.

These short comments should suffice to situate *The Family of Charles IV* among the masterpieces of Spanish painting. Here Goya demonstrates that he had attained his artistic maturity after his first attempts in this field in 1783, where incidentally he also included his own self-portrait. But we remarked above on the historical interest of the paintings that Goya carried out at Court: this one seems to be a subtle satire of the royal family, especially of the King and

133

Queen who preside over this array of solitary beings who seem like strangers to one another. Seldom has the feeling of loneliness in the midst of a crowd been more ably conveyed. The Queen stands aloof from the children whom she is touching. Still less motherly is the attitude of the princess who holds her baby. The King and Queen are totally detached from one another. Is it possible to catch a look of encouraging cordiality in the royal heir's expression? The only tender touches can be found in the childish faces of the princes Carlos María Isidro and Francisco de Paula, the first of whom was later to cause a serious struggle over the succession to the throne, which a son of the second ended in the next generation with his marriage to Ferdinand VII's daughter, Isabel II. All these faces can be examined again in a series of preliminary studies on display in the Prado.

Other portraits by Goya are also of historical interest, first and foremost that of *Manuel Godoy* (San Fernando Academy, Madrid), painted in 1801, with reminiscences of the recent military campaign against Portugal known in Spanish history as the "War of the Oranges". Godoy was obsessed by the idea of reigning over a tiny kingdom in the Algarve, which led him to sign a treaty with France and attack Portugal. These events are

The Marquise of Santa Cruz. *Louvre, Paris. Goya portrayed two sitters with this same title. This one was Maria Waldstein, born in Vienna in 1763 and married in 1791 to the widowed 9th Marquis of Santa Cruz. She was a highly cultured woman who became a member of the Royal Academy of San Fernando and even painted her own self-portrait which enabled art historian Jeannine Baticle to identify her in this portrait dating from around 1800.*

recalled in this portrait by the Portuguese flag. Charles IV's almighty favourite is portrayed in a reclining position and it is an open question whether Goya really intended to flatter him with this portrait. There is no doubt about it that he did not put the same accent on this work as did Velázquez when he painted his portrait of Philip IV's chief minister, the Duke of Olivares, on horseback. Here there is no clear intention to flatter, but rather a subtly ironic one. This is an unusual composition, broader than it is high and with lighting effects on a mountain background which is surprising in an artist who never showed much interest in landscapes.

By contrast we have the charming portrait of Godoy's wife, *The Countess of Chinchón*, daughter of the Infante Don Luis, whose position at Court was a very disheartening one. She had to endure the presence of her husband's mistress, Pepita Tudó, at table, although ironically her marriage to Godoy was intended to be a sign of her family's reinstatement after the ostracism to which Charles III had relegated her father. Goya put all his sympathy into this masterly portrait, painted in 1800, and also a certain degree of delicacy because the Countess was pregnant at the time and for this reason Goya portrayed her seated and drew attention to the mass and details of her dress. The composition is vaguely pyramid-shaped; the face appears rather too small in comparison with the long dress, but so melancholy and shy that in the end it catches and holds the viewer's attention. Golden tones predominate in the colour scheme and are skilfully graded in the draperies, flesh and hair colours and also in the background.

Another masterly portrait also dates from these early years of the 19th century, *The Marquise of Santa Cruz*, of which there are two versions. The best one, signed and dated 1805, was retrieved for the Prado in 1986. Previously it had been in the Valdés Collection in Bilbao, but was sold secretly and taken

Ferdinand Guillemardet. *Louvre, Paris. Apparently Goya was very satisfied with this portrait and considered it one of his best works. It combines fine pictorial quality and an informal composition. The sitter was born in 1765 and appointed French ambassador in Spain in 1798; the portrait was probably painted around that time. He was a member of the French Convention that condemned the king to death. He is known to have led intrigues in Spain with personalities belonging to Goya's circle of acquaintances. He died in 1809.*

abroad illegally (with false export documents). Later it came up for sale at a public art auction in London, where it could have fetched a fabulous price (over a thousand million pesetas); however, the Spanish government took legal action to avoid the sale and paid a considerable compensatory sum (of over eight hundred million pesetas) contributed by the State and private organisms, as a result of which the work returned to Spain and can now be admired in the Prado. It contains some details that are unique in Goya's artistic production. The sitter is Joaquina Téllez-Girón, one of the daughters of the Duke of Osuna, whom Goya had portrayed as a child with her

136

137

parents, brothers and sister in a portrait we mentioned earlier that can also be seen in the Prado. She was born in 1784 and died in 1851, having married her cousin the Marquis of Santa Cruz, José Gabriel de Silva Bazán, whose mother was also portrayed by Goya in a work in the Louvre. Joaquina holds a lyre with a swastika painted on it, which was the reason why this picture was nearly sent as a gift to Hitler early in the 1940s. Recalling this eventuality in 1952, Sánchez Cantón expressed his satisfaction that the portrait had remained in Spain, little suspecting the adventures that were to befall it a few decades later and the efforts and sacrifice required to bring it home again.

According to Gudiol, the *Marquise of Santa Cruz* is represented in the guise of Euterpe, the muse of lyrical poetry, with a crown of vine-leaves. In the Prado version a curl falls diagonally across her breast and she is wearing silk slippers. These are the details that differ from the other version, which Joseph Bonaparte wanted to take back to France and which later belonged to the Duke of Wellington. It was in the Los Angeles County Museum and later sold; although authentic, it is not of such fine quality as the one redeemed for the Prado. Commenting on this work's exceptional quality with respect to other portraits by Goya, Sánchez Cantón pointed out

Leandro Fernández de Moratín. Royal Academy of San Fernando, Madrid. He was the son of Nicolás Fernández de Moratín, a not very successful playwright and poet whose writings about the Inquisition and bull-fighting exerted an influence on Goya; Leandro was a close friend of Goya and probably the foremost figure of the Spanish Enlightenment in the literary field. Goya portrayed him on two occasions: the first time in 1799 in this excellent canvas and again in 1824 (Museum of Bilbao).

the relation between this picture and the two *"Majas"* and even the strange and little known female figure in *The Siesta* (Mac-Crohon Collection), which he called *The sleeping maja.*

An undated work that must have been painted around 1800 is the portrait of the *Marquise of Lazán,* an aunt of the Empress Eugenia of Montijo, which belongs to the Alba Collection in the Liria Palace in Madrid[46]. The pose is unusual (she

46. Her name was María Gabriela Palafox Portocarrero and she lived from 1779 to 1820. The title belonged to her husband, Luis Palafox, who was her cousin and also a brother of the famous general who defended Saragossa when the city was besieged during the Peninsular War.

is leaning against a chair), as is also the *chiaroscuro* colouring. About the same time Goya also painted portraits of *Francisca Sabasa García* and *The bookseller's wife*, both in the National Gallery, Washington. They reflect clearly enough how Goya's palette had become enriched in these early years of the 19th century, as can further be observed in his portrait of *Doña Isabel Cobos de Porcel* (National Gallery, London), painted in 1806, where the black mantilla provides a contrast to the green background and mauve tone of her dress[47].

---

47. Although these portraits are related from a stylistic point of view to the others considered so far, the sitters portrayed here represent a different social class. With regard to Francisca Sabasa García little is known about her except that she was the niece of the well-known politician Evaristo Pérez de Castro and married a certain Mr. Peñuelas from Toledo (see E. Du Gué Trapier, 1955). The *"Bookseller's wife of Carretas Street"*, according to art historian Sambricio (quoted by Gudiol, 1970, page 333), could have been the wife of Antonio Bailo, one of Goya's acquaintances, who had a bookshop in that street. Isabel Cobos de Porcel was the wife of the politician Antonio Porcel, who also had his portrait painted by Goya, although it was lost in the fire that destroyed the Jockey Club in Buenos Aires. Emilio Orozco (1966, pages 59-69) investigated the lady's biography. She was born in Ronda in Andalusia, although her father was from Extremadura and her mother from Seville. She married in 1802, at the age of 24, soon after her husband-to-be had become a widower. She had four children and apparently her interests lay in the field of art and literature.

Self-portrait. *Musée Goya, Castres, France. The date of this self-portrait, along with its replica (Bonnat Museum, Bayonne), is controversial. Art historian Gállego believes that Goya might have needed spectacles as a result of his serious illness in 1793. At all events Gállego points out that his mood in the two portraits is "melancholic and dejected".*

At this point we should pause for a moment to consider a series of miniature portraits that Goya painted around 1805 for the wedding of his son Javier to Gumersinda Goicoechea y Galarza. These miniatures measure 8 centimetres in diameter and have a copper frame; seven of them still exist in different collections, five of them female portraits, while the remaining two are of the artist's son and his father-in-law. The Prado purchased one representing *Juana Galarza de Goicoechea* (Javier's mother-in-law) which reveals Goya's skill in an unaccustomed field, using short quick brushstrokes to obtain a magnificent portrait[48].

---

48. Details about Goya's daughter-in-law and her family can be found in my work on Goya's miniatures (1980).

The Count of Fernán-Núñez.
Fernán-Núñez Collection, Madrid.
Art critic Gudiol rightly considered
this work of 1803 to mark a new
beginning in Goya's portraiture. It is
one of his most refined and elegant;
the head is superb. The sitter was
Carlos Gutiérrez de los Ríos, 7th
Count of Fernán-Núñez (1779-1822),
whom Goya had portrayed in a
conventional group with his parents,
brothers and sisters in 1787.

143

We should also turn our attention to a number of really masterly masculine portraits, beginning with another *Selfportrait* that used to be in the Count of Villagonzalo's collection and can now be viewed in the San Fernando Academy. Goya has portrayed himself in front of a canvas, with striking light effects because he is standing by a large window; the artist seems to be looking at a mirror without overdue attention to problems of poise or body proportions. However, these matters obviously concern him in two other magnificent works: the portraits of the *Count of Fernán Núñez* and the *Marquis of San Adrián*, painted in 1803 and 1804 respectively[49]. The former, wrapped in a cloak and standing with one leg in front of the other, his head turned slightly to the left, against a Velázquez-style landscape background, is portrayed in an elegant pose that reveals how our rough, unpolished painter was also capable of this type of refined portraiture that became typical of English painting after Van Dyck had worked at the Court of King Charles I. The same distinguished touch can be found in the second portrait: the Marquis of San Adrián

Doña Antonia Zárate. *Ermitage, Leningrad. The sitter belonged to a well-known family of actors and her son, Antonio Gil y Zárate, achieved fame as an author of historical dramas. The portrait was probably painted in 1810 during the Peninsular War. The actress died in 1811 at the age of 36. Her personal beauty is enhanced here by the elegance of the painting.*

is portrayed in a conventional manner, but with a sense of due proportion and balance, which his serene expression confirms.

During the French occupation from 1808 to 1814, when Spain was fighting for her political independence, part of Goya's artistic activities can be associated with the historical circumstances that Spain was going through. In this context the first work that occupies us is one of *Ferdinand VII on horseback* commissioned by the Royal Academy of San Fernando; there are numerous documents concerning its execution and payment. Goya received the commission only nine days after the so-called "Revolt of Aranjuez", which led to the abdication of Charles IV and proclamation of his son as King Ferdinand VII. It was painted between March 28th and October 2nd 1808, when war had already broken out. This type of

49. Regarding the Count of Fernán Núñez, see note 39. The Marquis of San Adrián was José M. de Magallón y Armendáriz. At the time he sat for Goya he had recently been made a grandee (1802); he died in 1845.

portrait appealed to Goya, although as we have seen he did not excel as a painter of animals. The bounding horse that the king is riding closely resembles the one that Velázquez painted in his equestrian portrait of Philip III. The landscape background also recalls Velázquez. The Museum of Agen in France has a preparatory sketch of this work.

We do not know what the portrait of Joseph Bonaparte was like that filled the oval medallion in Goya's *Allegory of Madrid*, commissioned by the Madrid City Council. Later we will come back to this work that was repainted several times and now only bears the words "Dos de Mayo" (2nd of May) in the medallion. Will X-rays one day be able to reveal the "intruder king's" features underlying the many coats of paint or have they disappeared completely, as Xavier de Salas suspected? However that may be, the fact is that thanks to this work Goya can go down as the painter of four kings.

During August and September 1812 the Duke of Wellington was in Madrid and Goya painted him on horseback. However, this large-scale canvas had originally been intended for a portrait of Godoy, as X-rays and certain documents published by Martínez Ripoll have proved. The equestrian portrait of *General Palafox*, dated 1814, closes

this cycle of portraits[50]. Others painted during this period are either of *"afrancesados"* or are more intimate portraits, revealing the different social standing of the sitters and how circumstances could influence the artist's attitude.

When Charles IV's son returned from France as king, Goya had little trouble in having his name removed from the political blacklist and soon resumed his work executing several portraits of *Ferdinand VII*. The most interesting of these are one in the Prado and another owned by the Santander City Council. It should be borne in mind that none of these portraits was painted by Goya in his capacity as Court Painter. They were all commissioned by different institutions or individual persons and therefore testify to a certain detachment from the Court on Goya's part, although the portrait in the Prado, where the king is portrayed in a long ermine cloak and holding the sceptre, has all the ingredients of a work intended for the Royal Palace. The one in

---

50. José Rebolledo de Palafox y Melci (1776-1847) was Captain General of Aragón during the Peninsular War and as such distinguished himself in the defence of Saragossa during the sieges of 1808 and 1809. After surrendering to the French troops in the 1809 siege he was taken to France as a prisoner and did not return until 1814. Ferdinand VII granted him the title of Duke of Saragossa.

General José de Palafox on horseback.
*Prado, Madrid. This is the second
portrait (painted in 1814) that Goya
made of the famous hero of the
Peninsular War. Although Goya was
not very expert at painting animals,
here, as Gudiol points out, the horse is
depicted with a lively forward
movement that gives the work an air
of general dynamism.*

Santander contains allegorical details that recall other allegories (particularly one in Stockholm) which might be related to the Constitution of 1812. The image that Goya conveys of Ferdinand VII in this period differs considerably from that of the large family portrait or even the equestrian portrait in the San Fernando Academy. The common feature now is the king's unpleasant expression. Goya only portrayed him once again and in a very distant manner in 1815 in his largest work (3.27 x 4.17 metres), where the king can be seen presiding over *The General Assembly of the Philippines Company* (Museum of Castres).

In 1815 he also painted two more self-portraits; one is now in the Prado and the other in the San Fernando Academy. Both reveal rapid brushwork and striking light contrasts. The face of the almost 70-year-old artist with his frank look is vigorously modelled. Goya has done away with the details that distracted his attention in his preceding works. These heads have a striking quality about them that has little in common with his earlier self-portraits. We must agree with Julián Gállego when he describes these two works as "astonishing" and worthy of Rembrandt. The portrait of *Mariano Goya* that belongs to the Duke of Albuquerque and bears the inscription "Goya to

Don Juan Bautista de Muguiro. *Prado, Madrid. This is one of the finest instances of Goya's creative talent. It bears an expressive dedication that ends with the words "...at the age of 81, in Bordeaux, May 1827". His old age was no obstacle to his working with a technique that art critic Sánchez Cantón considers "half a century ahead of his time, although this is often not admitted...; the deep colouring of the blue dress-suit and yellow upholstery seem to foreshadow the Manet to come".*

his grandson" on the reverse, was painted about the same time; it therefore serves as a contrast. The child is portrayed with a sheet of music in front of him; again the artist's fondness for children is evident, in this case his love for his son Javier's only child. Five years later we have another self-portrait in the rather strange painting of *Goya and his physician Dr. Arrieta* (Institute of Arts, Minneapolis). It bears the significant dedication: "From Goya out of gratitude to his friend Arrieta: for the skill and care with which he saved his life during the acute and dangerous illness he suffered at the end of 1819 at the age of 73. Painted in 1820."

Goya painted other portraits over these last years of his life that show how he progressed in technique and introduced innovations in his col-

ouring until the very end; these include *José Luis Munárriz* (1815, San Fernando Academy), the *Duke of San Carlos* (1815), the *10th Duke of Osuna* (1816, Bonnat Museum, Bayonne), the *Architect Tiburcio Pérez* (Metropolitan Museum, New York), *Don Ramón Satué* (1823,

Museum of Amsterdam), *Don Leandro Fernández de Moratín* (1824, Museum of Bilbao), *Mariano Goya* again, now a handsome young man (dedicated "Goya to his grandson in 1827 at the age of 81"), *Don Juan de Mugiro* (1827, Prado) and *José Pío de Molina* (1828, unfinished)[51]. In this period Goya applied the paint more thickly and preferred dark colours, ranging from blue to black. This series of portraits ends with one which proves to be the exception to the rule we have just mentioned as far as colour is concerned: *The milkmaid of Bordeaux* (Prado). She is portrayed in profile, leaning slightly forward, with almost square proportions and this work departs from those of the portrait gallery we have been commenting on, where the fundamental object was to reproduce the sitter's facial traits; here it is the painting as such that matters and the draperies are represented with short, varied strokes of colour. It is easy to understand why Sánchez Cantón considered that the technique used here contained hints of "neo-impressionism".

---

51. The circles in which Goya moved towards the end of his life can be deduced from this list of portraits. Luis Munárriz was the Secretary of the San Fernando Academy, although he resigned this post when he was appointed director of the Royal Philippines Company; his friendship with Goya was probably the reason why the latter was commissioned to paint the enormous Velázquez-style canvas representing one of the Company's meetings (as Sánchez Cantón suggested, 1951, page 109). The Duke of San Carlos was José Miguel de Carvajal y Vargas; he was born in Lima in 1771 and died in 1828. He accompanied Ferdinand VII to France. The portrait was commissioned by the Imperial Canal of Aragón and a preliminary sketch as well as a small-scale replica exist. Tiburcio Pérez Cuervo belonged to a family of architects from Asturias. He was born in Oviedo in 1792 and studied under his uncle Juan Antonio Cuervo, who had worked with the famous architect Ventura Rodríguez. The most important building he designed was the San Carlos College in Madrid, that was formerly the hospital of the old medical faculty. In connection with Pérez Cuervo's friendship with Goya, Sánchez Cantón (1951, page 124) recalled that he was required to act as Rosario Weiss' guardian when Goya left Madrid for Bordeaux. Ramón Satué was a magistrate in 1823. Juan Bautista Muguiro, born in 1786, was a banker from Navarra who is known to have been living in Bordeaux as a merchant after 1825. His brother José was Francisco Javier Goya's brother-in-law. He received a pass to travel to Madrid on

July 2nd 1827, which is possibly the reason why Goya painted his portrait before his departure from Bordeaux (see Núñez de Arenas, 1963, pages 226-227). José Pío Molina was the constitutional Mayor of Madrid in 1823.

The milkmaid of Bordeaux. *Prado, Madrid. Although it has not been dated with exactitude, this could have been Goya's last work. It was kept by Leocadia Zorrilla, the woman who looked after Goya until his death, and later purchased by his friend* *Juan de Muguiro (whose portrait he painted in 1827), possibly to help her financially. Pictorially it is surprising in its loose, fluid brushwork. The figure appears to be seated on a donkey. The canvas had been used previously.*

The clothed maja. The nude maja. The Marquise of Santa Cruz. *These three master-pieces are a landmark in Goya's production. Apart from their obvious artistic value they are also popular for other circumstances. In his* Episodios nacionales *the Spanish novelist Pérez Galdós related that the clothed maja covered the nude one in the Duchess of Alba's palace and the legend that the two paintings represent Cayetana de Alba has not been completely dismissed, although the face does not resemble that depicted in true portraits of the Duchess.* The nude maja *is known to have been hanging in Godoy's private rooms in his palace, along with other nudes, in 1800. But apart from all these conjectures, the three works marked Goya out as a painter of this type of female portraits in reclining poses, whose antecedent in Spanish art was Velázquez's* Rokeby Venus, *which Goya must have seen in the Alba palace before it was acquired by Godoy.*

The Majas

These paintings are probably Goya's most popular ones and have to some extent become symbolic of his work. They cannot be classified in any of the categories we have set up, although they could be considered portraits of someone. Thanks to the art historian Pardo Canalis we know that *The nude maja* had been painted by 1800; it is the one described in Godoy's collection as "A nude (Venus) by Goya, without draughtsmanship nor grace nor colouring". *The clothed maja* is not mentioned in this list, which justifies Xavier de Salas' opinion that it was painted at a later date.

All this does not in any way confirm the popular belief that the two majas represent the Duchess of Alba. Godoy put the nude one side

by side with Velázquez's *Rokeby Venus*, which the famous Duchess had already given him by 1800, two years before her death. The three works, i.e. Goya's two majas and Velázquez's masterpiece, figured in the inventory of 972 works in Godoy's possession on January 1st 1808.

The nude maja and Velázquez's Venus are the two great exceptions

153

in Spanish art, which owing to its preoccupation with religious subjects ignored a field of painting that had produced splendid works, like those of Titian and Rubens, many of which were included in the royal collection. Goya's picture offers a direct, spontaneous image of the model, although Sotomayor remarked that the head seems to fit the body in an artificial manner. Obviously this nude offsets Velázquez's mythological figure as if it were intended as a deliberate contrast. The sensually nonchalant posture of Goya's maja is the reverse of Velázquez's Venus who decorously turns her back to the spectator. The influence of Goya's work on Manet's *Olympia* is obvious.

In comparison, *The clothed maja* makes us admire Goya's use of bold brushstrokes to set off the details of the draperies clinging to her body. If indeed the work did not exist in 1800, it cannot be dated much later. The pose recalls the two versions of the *Marquise of Santa Cruz* that Goya painted in 1805. And if we want to trace derivations we could refer to the sleeping young girls that he had depicted in the last decade of the previous century (Mac-Crohon Collection, Madrid, and National Gallery, Dublin).

The fall. *Private collection, Madrid. This is one of a series of seven canvases with anecdotal subjects painted for the Alameda de Osuna country palace in 1787. It is one of the liveliest and possibly represents a real event that occurred to the Duchesses of Alba and Osuna, although the landscape does not correspond to the Osuna estate.*

From the likeness of reality to the "Dreams of reason"

Goya interpreted everyday reality in so-called genre paintings which we began to examine in the chapter on his tapestry cartoons, where he depicted popular scenes illustrating typical habits and customs of Madrid life. In this context we already mentioned that this type of subject-matter did not originate with Goya; it belonged to the atmosphere of 18th-century art and explains why certain Flemish painters' works (for example, Teniers and Brouwers) came to life again in

tapestries. However, themes of this kind made a very special impact on our painter's sensibility, which is reflected in his works. He fell back on this branch of painting time and time again during his life, not only on canvas, but also in drawings and etchings. His changes in temperament can be followed by observing the kind of topics he preferred at each point and the technique he chose to interpret them. Certain crucial moments in his life are reflected in his choice of themes, which became a refuge in times of solitude, when his imagination ran away with him. Thus in his paintings, as well as in his drawings and etchings to be considered at the end of this book, Goya ended up using an artistic language in which, to quote one of his own titles, "the dream of reason brings forth monsters".

During the period of his activity for the Royal Tapestry Manufactory Goya painted several small pictures whose subject-matter ran parallel to those of his tapestry designs. Let us return to the fine sketch he prepared (which was never reproduced as a full-size cartoon) of *St. Isidore's Meadow* with all the bustle of the saint's feast-day. This wide composition is reminiscent, as we already mentioned, of Velázquez's *View of Saragossa*, with figures distributed on different planes in the foreground, behind them the river

Strolling players. *Prado, Madrid. The subject of this work is unusual in Goya's production. It probably recalls the Italian* Commedia dell' Arte. *The abbreviated inscription in the lower left corner is generally supposed to stand for* alegoria menandrea *(as the actors' tribute to the Greek poet Menander). The figures on the stage are Colombine, Harlequin, Pantaloon and the clown, as well as a dwarf. The work might have belonged to a series of "cabinet pictures" that Goya painted after his illness in 1793 and offered to the Royal Academy of San Fernando.*

and in the background the outline of the city. He has achieved an extraordinary impression of liveliness and movement among the groups, with careful draughtsmanship in those closer to the viewer and colour outlining of the more distant ones. The works he painted for the Osuna palace in La Alameda, now dispersed in various different collections, date from the same year (1787). The most famous and

attractive ones, that belonged to the Duke of Montellano, are: *The swing*, a subject he had already painted in a tapestry cartoon, *A stage-coach held up by bandits*, with anecdotic details in the scenes of the passengers and the robbers, *The fall*, which Ezquerra del Bayo interpreted as a true incident that befell the Duchesses of Osuna and Alba, and finally *The greased pole*, that depicts two boys climbing a pole to reach a prize hanging at the top. In the 1790s Goya's manner of interpreting these genre scenes changed considerably. In 1794 he presented a set of "cabinet pictures" to the Academy which he had executed during his serious illness "to occupy my imagination mortified by my ailing health", in his own words. These comprised eleven pictures, to which he intended to add four more, although these have not been identified.

In an interesting study Xavier de Salas tried to revive the atmosphere of these "cabinet pictures" where Goya "made observations that cannot normally be expressed in commissioned works, which offer no scope for flights of fancy or inventiveness". The identification of some of the subjects is controversial, but in general these small-size ($\pm$ 46 $\times$ 31 centimetres) paintings on tin reflect a reality that Goya often interprets with an extremely critical intention. These comprise, among others: *The*

There they go fleeced. *Prado, Madrid. Preparatory sketch in sanguine for etching no. 20 of the* Caprichos. *The Prado also has another sketch that differs in that it is inverted and contains railings that alter the light effect. The title refers to the way in which prostitutes dismiss their clients after stripping them of their money, while two monks look on in a "pious" attitude.*

lunatics' courtyard, Strolling players, Bandits holding up a stage-coach, Shipwreck, Fire, Inside a prison, as well as some bullfight scenes.

This series of "cabinet pictures" marks a new period in Goya's art as far as subject-matter is concerned. *The lunatics' courtyard* (Virginia Meadows Museum, Dallas, Texas) is mentioned in a letter that Goya wrote to the vice-director of the Academy, Bernardo de Iriarte, and its poignant tone can act as an introduction to the whole series. *The strolling players* (Prado), on the other hand, has a gay touch to it with the performers moving about the stage. *Fire* (Plácido Arango Collection, Madrid) should be mentioned as a forerunner of Géricault's *Raft of the "Medusa"*.

The Prado has two small pictures on tin of very similar measurements. One is *The slaying*, which shows a nude woman trapped by a man with a knife who seems to be about to cut her throat; the other is called *The bonfire* and depicts several nude men around the blaze of a fire. Relating the type of subject-matter, size and material used one is tempted to include these two pictures in the series that Goya presented to the Academy. It is rather surprising that there are also versions on wood of these two subjects, although they are generally considered to be of a later date: Gudiol dates them around 1800, whereas Gassier and Wilson attribute them to the time of the Peninsular War (1808-1814).

During his stay in Sanlúcar de Barrameda Goya made a series of satirical drawings, which were subsequently engraved, together with others, giving rise to the so-called *Caprichos* in 1800. The difference in subject-matter between these quick sketches and the afore-mentioned paintings cannot be more striking. But since we are now dealing with his paintings we will only point out that after these first attempts Goya painted much more freely in the works he executed from 1798 onwards. This was the year he carried out the frescoes in San Antonio de la Florida. The same year he also painted several

Flagellants' procession. The Madhouse. *Royal Academy of San Fernando, Madrid. These two works belong to a group of four with the same measurements whose common characteristics are a stirringly dramatic handling and short, lively brushstrokes. They were bequeathed to the Academy in 1839, but it is not known when they were painted. They are generally considered to date from the time of the Peninsular War (1808-1814). During those years Goya painted a number of small-scale works with a pungently critical intention, possibly as the result of a personal experience similar to that of 1792-3 when he suffered the illness that deprived him of his hearing, after which he painted a series of "cabinet pictures" where he could freely develop his "flights of fancy and inventiveness". Here his critical sense becomes more biting as he portrays the penitents with their bare backs or the mentally deranged in their crowded asylum. The outdoor procession is depicted with completely different light effects to the indoor scene in the madhouse that seems more like a sordid prison. The colouring is also different in the two pictures. But the general haunting impression is the same in both. The other two works of this series represent* The Court of the Inquisition *and* A bullfight.

small pictures of *Witchcraft*, which are the first samples of a theme that he was to enlarge on twenty years later, but with the difference that in time these themes took on an expressionistic turn that was lacking at the start. His increasingly loose technique with its splashes of colour seems to stress this atmosphere that gradually lost all sense of proportion of everyday reality. However, since contradictions are the general rule with Goya, at the same time he was capable of painting a series of optimistic works like *The seasons* and other subjects similar to his tapestry cartoons for the Osuna family's country palace in La Alameda. The sketch of *St. Isidore's Meadow* which he supposedly made ten years earlier has also sometimes been referred to in connection with these reduced versions...

Passing over several years we come to the eve of the Peninsular War, when Goya painted the cycle of six works now in the Museum of Chicago on *The capture of the bandit Maragato by Fray Pedro de Zaldivia*, based on a real incident that happened in 1806. The war must have made Goya take refuge in himself to escape from outside events that were troubling his mind; he executed five notable small paintings on wood, now in the San Fernando Academy, which allow us a glimpse of his so-called

Making gun-powder in the Sierra de Tardienta. Making bullets in the Sierra de Tardienta. La Zarzuela Palace, Madrid. Similar comments could be made about these two small-scale works (only 33 cm. high) to those made on the preceding page about the pictures in the Royal Academy, except that these bear the identifying inscription "Gun-powder (or bullet) works run by Don Josep Mallen in the Sierra de Tardienta in Aragón in the years 1811, 1812 and 1813". Both scenes are depicted with extraordinary naturalism, as if Goya had witnessed them, great vigour in the colouring and liveliness in the figures, achieved by means of precise brush-strokes. Observe, for example, the fire in the second picture. Art critics have pointed out the similarity between the figure with his back to the viewer in this picture and the blacksmith in The forge *(Frick Collection, New York).*

"wild-veined" aspect. This expression is especially well applied in the context of the *Bullfight in a village*, which is a masterly piece of painting, not only in its subject-matter, but in particular owing to its loose brushwork and bold splashes of colour. As far as technique is concerned Goya had by then completely broken away from Neoclassical rules. In this picture, apart from the principal figures in the bullfight arena, the spectators catch

162

our attention: some of the groups are outlined with energetic strokes of ink and others are indicated with softly diffused colour stains. Here again contrasting pictorial devices are combined to produce vibrating effects. In another work, *The burial of the sardine*, Goya applied this "expressionistic" technique to the masked figures, thus giving them a rather dramatic air.

In these critical years Goya laid bare his spiritual and ideological position in paintings that introduce us to a much more harrowing world. These are scenes concerning the Inquisition, which were probably inspired by his friend, the canon and historian of this court, Juan Antonio Llorente, of whom he also painted an excellent portrait. It cannot be denied that this man was as one-sided in his judgements as the Inquisition itself, with which he was perfectly acquainted since he was responsible for its archives when the institution was suppressed in 1809. About this time Goya painted *The Court of the Inquisition*, where the accused in their tall pointed caps emphasize the gloominess of the scene. These figures cannot be considered victims of contemporary procedures of the Holy Office, which by Goya's time no longer went about its business in this manner, but he exaggerated the melodramatic mood of the picture owing to his logical resentment

The burial of the sardine. Royal Academy of San Fernando, Madrid. This panel belongs to a bequest to the Academy, but its measurements differ from those of the other four in the same institution, although this is possibly due to the requirements of the subject, because in style they are extremely similar. It is therefore to be assumed that they also date from the years of the Peninsular War. Here again we come across Goya's so-called "wild vein". The scene reflects a mixture of light-hearted merry-making and wild lack of restraint. The Prado has a preparatory sketch with variations.

against the institution. The fact that the Inquisition had taken action against Goya for producing the *Caprichos* and *The nude maja* should not be overlooked. From a purely pictorial point of view, the "almost Rembrandtesque" effects of light, to quote one critic, are interesting in this panel.

A more realistic and vibrating image of Spain in Goya's time can be found in the *Flagellants' procession*, which shows figures of penitents with flagellated backs, illustrating a form of devotion that was subsequently reflected in works by José Gutiérrez Solana (1886-1945). *The Madhouse* is the last of

this cycle. Here, as in the Inquisition scene, although in paler colours, the play of lighting effects on these poor, half-naked lunatics is important. Along the same lines, *The hospital for the plague-stricken* (owned by the Marquis de la Romana) is the most Rembrandt-esque of all in its interpretation of light, which falls on the scene from the rear leaving the dying figures in the foreground in the shade.

Leaving aside several other pictures painted during the war, which although genre in subject-matter can best be commented on in the context of their historical connections, we come to *Young girls on a balcony*. It is a theme that Goya repeated in several replicas and was widely imitated in the 19th century by artists like Manet and Eugenio Lucas. The type of composition and subject-matter are directly related to typical tapestry designs. But its extraordinarily advanced technique leads us to date the most famous version, the one in the Metropolitan Museum of New York, around this time.

During the last decades of his life Goya continued to be interested in everyday scenes, which he interpreted with an increasingly free technique and a colour scheme full of contrasts where finally grey and black tones predominate. *The water-carrier* and *The knifegrinder*

Scene from "El Lazarillo de Tormes" Araoz Collection, Madrid. Its previous owner, the famous doctor Marañón (who willed it to his daughter), believed this work to represent an old-fashioned cure for croup or diphtheria. However the true explanation of the scene has been discovered thanks to the marking X 25 in the lower right-hand corner, that corresponded to a painting entitled El Lazarillo de Tormes in the inventory drawn up after Goya's wife died in 1812 and left to the artist's son. Style-wise it belongs to the years of the war. Observe the effect of light on the flesh tones and sketchily painted shirts, as well as the fire. The scene illustrates a 16th-century novel about the pranks of a blind man's guideboy (Lazarillo). Here the boy has eaten his master's sausage instead of cooking it for him and the blind man discovers the trick by sticking his nose into the boy's mouth.

(Museum of Budapest) are full of life. *The forge* (Frick Collection, New York) offers a very direct scene of several men at work around the anvil. In *Inside a prison* (Monastery of Guadalupe), which was left to Javier Goya in 1812, Goya depicts a dramatic scene similar to others he touched on in his drawings, which could be related in date and technique to the scene from *"El Lazarillo de Tormes"* reproduced on the following page.

166

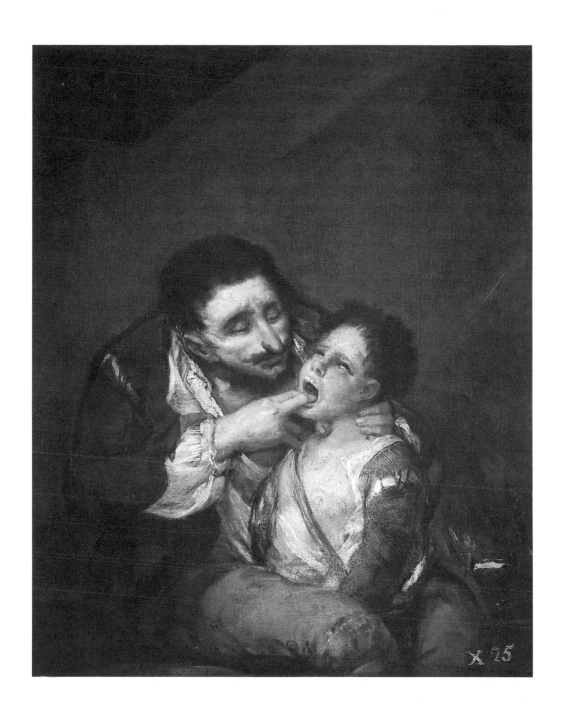

From myths and allegories to the turmoils of history

Here we have to do with a branch of painting that acquired growing importance in Goya's art although certain aspects of this type of subject-matter did not correspond to the artist's sensibility. Depicting the past or reviving mythological fables obliges a painter to create artificial compositions and this is what did not suit the temperament of a man who preferred to examine reality in a direct manner; this approach was incompatible with inventing make-believe versions of historical events on canvas or paper. Nevertheless, we can now go on to see how in Goya's artistic output there is also scope for historical paintings (with particular emphasis on events he had actually witnessed), allegories and mythological subjects.

In the first place his initial "failures" at the Academy must be mentioned. For the scholarship examinations in 1763 and 1766 he had to represent *The Empress Martha of Constantinople interceding with Alfonso the Wise on behalf of her husband Baldwin* and *The Dispute between Juan de Urbina and Diego de Paredes for the arms*

of the Marquis of Pescara. Without doubt Goya must have been happier painting on his own initiative two pictures on the topical subject of *The Riot against Esquilache* in 1766 (See Pita, 1989). A few years later we find Goya in Italy carrying out small-scale paintings to earn his living. Two of these are in the Gudiol Collection in Barcelona: *Sacrifice to Vesta* and *Sacrifice to Pan*. With their Roman atmosphere and suggestion of classical monuments they conform to Neo-classical norms.

His return to Spain and his work in Saragossa and for the Royal Tapestry Manufacture led Goya to con-

Commerce. Industry. Agriculture. Prado, Madrid. These three tondos belonged to a series of four that once adorned Godoy's palace, which is rather significant considering their "enlightened" character. They might date from the last years of the 18th century. The fourth tondo was an allegory of Science, but it can be regarded as lost since it was completely repainted. Goya uses Oriental-looking (Turkish?) figures to represent Commerce, Flora with flowers and fruit for Agriculture, whereas Velázquez-style weavers symbolize Industry.

centrate on a different kind of subject-matter, although the work believed to represent *The Sacrifice of Iphigenia* (Varez Fisa Collection, San Sebastián), dating from the period 1775-1780, according to Gudiol, is, in style, a late echo of his stay in Italy. This painting has also been interpreted as a biblical subject: the sacrifice of Jephthah's daughter.

Apart from mythological themes it should also be remembered that in 1771 he sent a work to the Academy of Parma representing *Hannibal contemplating Italy from the Alps*, identified by Prof. Rogelio Buendía, which Goya painted in compliance with the requirements of an academic competition. All the canvases mentioned should be considered more from the point of view of Goya's education as a painter than for their own artistic value. Subsequently, when heroes of the antique world occasionally appear in his works, it is in a critical or satirical connection, for example *Hercules and Omphale*, which he painted in a burlesque tone in 1784 or *Saturn* in the Black Paintings towards the end of his life, which he interpreted in expressionistic terms.

The sketches and canvases for Valencia Cathedral also have something historical about them in that they record episodes of the life of St. Francis Borgia, although in this case they are intended to reflect a religious context. In particular the one depicting the saint taking leave of his family is painted in a historical manner, with great attention to costume and even a melodramatic touch in some of the family members' sad mood or tears; Sánchez Cantón pointed out that the figures are dressed in the style of Philip III's time, almost a century after the correct date. The same critic also referred to Goya's intention of painting a work on *The Surrender of Seville*, in this context of history paintings, as well as certain historical implications such as allusions to the Cid or Charles V in his bullfight scenes. But all this lies beyond the scope of this book. Some of the portraits already mentioned, like *The Family of Charles IV* or *Manuel Godoy* after the war against Portugal, could also be considered genuine history paintings.

Around the turn of the century Goya painted a number of curious pictures that introduce us to the world of allegory, another branch that he embarked on in his urge to try his hand on almost every kind of subject-matter. When we come to his drawings and etchings we will have the opportunity of commenting on various original themes of the *Caprichos* that include allegorical details. But for the moment we will concentrate on several allegories in oils.

The 2-metre wide tondos with allegories of *Commerce, Industry, Agriculture* and *Science* must have been painted before 1800. They were intended for the main staircase of Godoy's palace (which now, after many alterations, forms part of the present-day Senate building). Hardly anything remains of the last one, but the other three are displayed in the Prado; in spite of their swift execution they reveal a certain interest in light and spatial effects. The allegorical intention is barely perceivable. Those representing *Commerce* and *Industry* consist of interiors with figures writing and two weavers, whereas *Agriculture* is symbolized by a female figure with a crown of ears of wheat next to a male figure bearing a basketful of fruit.

The beginning of the 19th century reveals a new vein: in the whole of Goya's work it is difficult to find such a complex process in creating a picture as that which led up to his *Allegory of the 1812 Constitution*. This process was surmised in 1945 by Sánchez Cantón and very ingeniously construed by Eleanor A. Sayre in 1979. An exhibition held in Madrid in 1982 contributed towards clearing up doubts and confirming a number of hypotheses. In short, the facts are as follows. About 1798 Goya made a sanguine drawing representing *Time and Truth*, the former symbolized by a

winged figure of Chronos holding an hour-glass, while the latter is portrayed nude walking behind Time, whose hand she holds. On the reverse of this drawing is a wash study of a female nude that reappears in a small canvas now in the Museum of Boston showing *Truth saved by Time with History as a witness*. The same two nude figures of the sanguine drawing appear again here full-face and holding hands, but Truth is portrayed in a static position like in the wash sketch; in the foreground and also nude History can be seen writing. This oil painting of about 1798, as well as the drawing, were in the artist's workshop until his wife Josefa's death in 1812. When the estate was divided up they were left to the couple's only living son, Francisco Javier. This circumstance possibly caused Goya to reconsider the allegory which he had taken into account when he painted the one dedicated to the "intruder king" Joseph Bonaparte, as we shall see later. But this small picture in the Boston Museum inspired a fine painting now in the Museum of Stockholm which was probably intended to commemorate the first democratic constitution drafted by the Spanish people. In this final version the previous figure of Truth has been transformed into a female figure clothed in a low-necked garment holding a small book in one hand and a sceptre in the other; the

Truth saved by Time with History as a witness. *Museum of Fine Arts, Boston.* Allegory of the Constitution. *Nationalmuseum, Stockholm. These two paintings, together with a preparatory sketch of the first one, are interesting examples of Goya's artistic development. At the end of the century Goya painted a small canvas* *depicting Chronos, the god of Time, hand in hand with a nude female figure symbolizing Truth, while another figure representing History is writing. After 1812 this scene was redone on a large scale and transformed into a matronly figure holding a sceptre and a book symbolizing the Constitution.*

format of the book is not merely artistic licence because at the time the Constitution was apparently also published in small-size editions. The figure of Chronos resembles that of the sketch, as does the figure symbolizing History, although from the waist down she is now covered in draperies. With this large-scale (almost 3-metre high) allegory Goya not only intended to paint a memorial to an important liberal event, but also to carry out a major work, as can be observed in the fine chromatic values of the flesh colours and the pearly tones of Time's wings and the draperies of the matronly figure symbolizing the Constitution.

Dated in 1810, the *Allegory of the City of Madrid* was therefore painted two years before the Stockholm canvas. Here a clothed female figure, which could be described as half-way between the nude symbol of Truth and the clothed Constitution, represents the city of Madrid: her right arm rests on a stone slab with the coat-of-arms of Madrid and her left hand points to an oval medallion held by two angels. In this medallion Goya originally painted Joseph Bonaparte's portrait, which was covered after the French withdrew from Madrid in August 1812 and inscribed with the word "Constitution". When Joseph I returned in November his portrait was restored, but in June of the following year Goya was paid to replace the venerable word; however, after Ferdinand VII returned and abolished the Constitution in May 1814 a poor-quality bust-length portrait of the new king was made to fill the oval space, which had to be repainted in 1826 by the renowned portraitist Vicente López (1772-1830). In 1843 the king's features were replaced by the book of the Constitution and finally, in 1872, another painter, Palmaroli, gave it its present-day appearance with the words "Dos de Mayo" (May 2nd). Apart from the angels holding the medallion, in the upper part of the picture there are two more angels, one blowing a trumpet and the other bearing a laurel wreath. These angels probably owe something to those in the San Antonio de la Florida frescoes, although the one with the trumpet is directly derived from the Chronos figure in the picture in Boston.

But Goya's allegories go further. When he was commissioned to paint a portrait of Ferdinand VII for the city of Santander in 1814, he resorted to the symbolic figure of the Constitution to represent Spain. The hand holding the book of the Constitution in the previous picture (the Boston allegory) is now hidden behind the king's head. It is difficult to resist wondering whether Goya's Maquiavellian idea was to show how the Constitution was now

174

The colossus *or* Panic. *Prado, Madrid. It is difficult to interpret this work, which was painted during or immediately after the Peninsular War. Does the giant half turned away from the viewer represent Napoleon on the other side of the Pyrenees? Whatever he is intended to symbolize,* he offers a contrast to the small people and animals scattering in all directions (with the exception of a single donkey that stands unperturbed) presumably terrified at the sight of the threatening figure looming up through the clouds.*

concealed by the head of the man who had abolished it.

During the war Goya's works reflect the upheavals his country was going through. In his drawings, sketches and canvases it is only too easy to discern that he was in the throes of the most serious moral crisis of his life. All these circumstances that were affecting him so closely are significantly recorded in his works. Without going into his personal standpoint the enormous interest of the series entitled *Disasters of War* as a testimony of the tragic events should be stressed. If Goya had occasionally turned to genre scenes as a means of escaping from other preoccupations, in these drawings he gave vent to his feelings of despair with regard to the Spanish people's unequal struggle against the French troops, brought to a head in his case by his personal attitude towards the positive ideological implications of the invasion. The *Disasters of War* are therefore a formidable outburst against war in general. There is no intention of taking sides or dividing the two camps into the "right" and "wrong" side. It is true that the *Disasters* exalt the patriotism of the Spanish people, but their real intention is to bear witness to the dramatic events which involved the Peninsula as a whole.

The most direct interpretation of historical events is to be found in

The aerostatic balloon. *Museum of Agen, France. This work belonged to Javier Goya. Art historian Jeannine Baticle considers it related to* The colossus, *although here there is no helter-skelter movement but only the motion of the dark horses contrasting with the white one standing still. As in* The colossus, *the landscape is an imaginary one. It is not known whether any particular balloon ascent is alluded to in this work. Although it is difficult to imagine that it reflects any event of the Peninsular War, it probably dates from that period.*

Goya's sketches. But several paintings should also be included in this period (1808-1814). Two of them are in the Zarzuela Palace in Madrid: they depict *Making gunpowder* and *Making bullets in the Sierra of Tardienta* (Aragón), according to their inscription. Another is *The Colossus* or *Panic* (Prado), which is impressively dramatic; it represents a gigantic figure emerging from clouds and towering over a valley where men and animals flee panic-stricken in all directions. Only a lone donkey remains unmoved in its place. Whom or what does the giant symbolize? Most probably Napoleon himself wrecking havoc in Spain, although Nigel Glendinning also put forward the theory that it could

176

be the spirit of Spain threatening over the Pyrenees. It is a composition full of forcefully realistic scenes. Technically it reveals vigorous contrasts between the splashes of colour indicating the silhouettes in motion down in the valley and the fluid modelling of the Herculean figure above.

But the epitome of Goya's outbursts against war can be found in his famous paintings commemorating the events of May 1808 in Madrid: *The Charge of the Mamelukes in the Puerta del Sol on May 2nd* and *The Executions on Príncipe Pío hill on May 3rd*. It is difficult to imagine a more vivid and vibrating testimony of these tragic incidents and logically there have been many conjectures as to whether Goya actually witnessed them. On the one hand he was believed to have been living in a house near the famous Puerta del Sol, but this notion was rejected in a study by the historian Gámir. On the other hand the writer Trueba narrated an unlikely tale by one of Goya's servants who alleged having accompanied his master to the Príncipe Pío hill before daybreak to contemplate the bodies of the executed patriots. It will never be known how much belongs to reality and how much to the realms of fantasy in these famous paintings, nor is it relevant, since what is really essential here is that they are the fruit of emotions and ex-

periences far stronger than any visual impressions. It is somewhat surprising to know that these two canvases were not painted until six years after the events took place. In February 1814 Goya expressed his desire to "perpetuate by means of the brush the most memorable and heroic episodes of our glorious uprising...". He wrote this, it must be remembered, at a time when he needed to proclaim his patriotism after the hesitating attitude he had adopted regarding the "intruder king" Joseph Bonaparte; several months later he had to face an inquiry at the Academy and at Court for political liability. He began the mentioned project with these two paintings. Surely he also planned to commemorate the defence of the city of Saragossa with Agustina de

Aragón, because there are preliminary sketches of the heroine standing next to a cannon. The two works depicting the uprising in Madrid were presumably meant to be the starting point of a cycle he never completed since chronologically they refer to events that triggered off the war and occurred in the capital. Beruete's suggestion that they could have been used to adorn a triumphal arch erected for Ferdinand VII's entry in Madrid on May 7th 1814 is quite possible. This would explain the rapid technique that seems to presage that of present-day posters.

Although they were not painted until 1814, these works were undoubtedly imagined during the war, probably shortly after the incidents took place. Sketches in the Duke of Villahermosa's collection in Madrid and in the Hispanic Society of America in New York seem to confirm this, as well as the fact that the 1812 inventory of Goya's estate lists twelve paintings of scenes illustrating "the horrors of the war" which, according to Sánchez Cantón, could include eight violent genre scenes now in the collection of the Marquis de la Romana.

Like in a snapshot, *The Charge of the Mamelukes* depicts a moment of fierce struggle between the people of Madrid attacking the Napoleonic troops (here Egyptian Mamelukes) dispatched to put an end to the uprising. The groups are positioned in disorder, with no attention to academic norms. Details are so vigorously stressed that they command the viewer's interest more than the composition as a whole, especially because of their expressive colouring. Goya realized the effects he could achieve by juxtaposing tones instead of blending them and of modifying true colours to obtain specific pictorial results. For this reason he does not hesitate to use green for a horse's head.

Goya's interpretation of the execution scene is unprecedented in the history of art in its intensely dramatic content. It centres around the figures of the men facing the firing squad. Time stands still for an agonizing instant, while the dead bodies of the executed cover the foreground and the condemned await their turn. The expressions of each of the men opposite the firing squad reflect different emotions. This is not the exaltation of heroic men fearlessly giving up their lives, but the much more human and intense emotion of those who go to their death because there is no other way out. These men facing their executioners are not preparing to sacrifice their lives for their country; their lives are being taken from them on her behalf. In view of this terrible truth, the soldiers are irrel-

evant; they are portrayed like shadows, from behind, while the light focuses on the condemned men and in particular on the central figure with his outstretched arms, pure white shirt and yellow trousers, colours that are echoed in the lantern. Traces of this scene can be found again from Manet (*The Execution of the Emperor Maximilian*) down to Picasso (*Massacre in Korea*); it has been decisive in interpreting similar scenes in art, not only in the manner of representing them, but also in its vibrating colours and light effects, that presage Impressionism.

May 3rd 1808 in Madrid: the executions on Príncipe Pío hill. *Prado, Madrid. Here death is portrayed in the most gripping manner. None of the versions considered antecedents or offshoots of this pathos-laden scene can match it in its superb representation of Time: past (the dead bodies on the ground), the present moment (the last instant of desperate expectancy) and future (the men lined up before the firing squad). All this is expressed in a vibrant pictorial language, using juxtaposed brush-strokes in the same way the Impressionists were to do later.*

A final strange example of Goya's history painting is his enormous picture of *The General Assembly of the Philippines Company* (Musée Goya, Castres, France), presided over by Ferdinand VII; there is a preparatory sketch in the Dahlem Museum, Berlin. It dates from about 1815. Art critic López Rey discovered some similarities in the atmosphere of this work and that of Velázquez's *Meninas* (or *Maids of Honour*). Although Goya's composition is much more rigid (a rectangular space, where the presiding members of the board are seated at a table in the background with a number of other figures on both sides of the room), the way in which the light falls on the scene from the right is reminiscent of Velázquez's spatial effects.

The Black Paintings

The works known as the "Black Paintings" covered the walls of two rooms, one on the ground floor and another on the first floor, of the country house that Goya bought in 1819 near the River Manzanares. They were transferred to canvas and given to the Prado in the last century and since they were cleaned the description "black" is not quite so fitting; however, considering their morbid content and bold technique the term is no doubt aptly applied. They were carried out between February 1819 and Goya's departure from Spain in June 1824. Possibly they were painted in the summer months, maybe during the so-called "three-year constitutional period" that raised such high hopes in Goya and other liberal-minded Spaniards, starting in March 1820, when Ferdinand VII was obliged to take the oath on the Constitution, only to come to a bitter end in 1823 when he called in French troops, declared null and void all the constitutional government's resolutions and re-established absolutist rule. Art historian Xavier de Salas suggested 1823 as the most probable date. The fact is that they are the work of a man well over seventy at the end of an intense life full of experiences that caused him to view the world around him in the most devastating terms and introduce disturbing symbols in his works. These disconcerted his critics; when the paintings were donated to the Prado in the past century they were considered at first unworthy of being displayed there and their apparent lack of a coherent iconographic pattern was criticized. In our times art historians such as Angulo, Nordström, Glendinning, López Vázquez and in particular Santiago Sebastián have all endeavoured to unravel the mystery of their hidden meaning.

Fantastic vision (Asmodeus). Two men fighting with clubs. *Prado, Madrid. Goya painted these two works on the walls of the upper room of the "Quinta del Sordo", which he purchased in 1819. The meaning of these "Black Paintings" is extremely hard to construe, if indeed they had one. Apart from the difficulty of interpreting them, there is also the important fact, disclosed by X-rays, that originally all these paintings were simply landscapes and that the subject-matter was painted in later. So in the first place the scenery should be contemplated. In the picture with two figures floating in the air, the imposing rocky mass commands attention and serves as a contrast to the trail of horsemen and the two soldiers levelling their rifles. In the other scene the wide open valley with mountains has completely lost its peaceful mood with the addition of these two struggling figures.*

Taking Saturn as his starting point Diego Angulo stated in 1962 that "these paintings were imagined and construed according to a central idea". Simultaneously Nordström carried out an extensive study on this subject centred on the same mythological figure and melancholy. Glendinning found a kind of humanistic explanation in 1978, which was the basis of Santiago Sebastián's interesting hypotheses in 1979, followed by José Manuel López Vázquez's Neo-platonic interpretation in 1981. But all these are conjectures that by no means offer a conclusive explanation of the meaning behind these paintings.

The popular belief that these Black Paintings dated from the years of the war and that Goya was living in the "Quinta del Sordo" (its name, "Deaf Man's Villa", had nothing to do with the artist) already in May 1808, including Antonio de Trueba's tale about Goya and his servant walking from there up to the Príncipe Pío hill to see the bodies of the executed, was refuted in 1946 by Sánchez Cantón on the basis of documents. The cycle has to be dated later, which heightens Goya's merits by revealing him capable of such an extraordinary creative effort at the age of almost seventy-seven.

The series comprises fourteen different-sized paintings, six of which covered the walls of a very large room (almost 9 metres by over $5\frac{1}{2}$ metres) on the ground floor, the other eight being situated in an equally large room upstairs. They were painted in oils directly on the plaster and when Baron Frederic Emile d'Erlanger purchased the villa in 1860 he had them transferred to canvas, giving them to the Prado twenty years later.

Since he painted them as murals, directly on the walls, it is correct to suppose that Goya must have set up some scheme for each room before starting work, although without giving up his freedom of expression and always leaving ample scope for improvisation as he went along, following a sudden impulse or flash of inspiration, because few artists were as loath to abide by a pre-established plan as Goya. Imagined and executed in the artist's ripe old age, these Black Paintings show how the process of artistic creation involves mysterious stages that the viewer or critic can best grasp by concentrating on the most external signs. We will never be able to lay Goya's soul bare and discover the innermost workings of his mind that made him give life to monstrous beings, witches, mythological and biblical figures or just plain mortals on the walls of his house. The most contradictory subjects were made to coexist here in these rooms and when we refer to a

Fantastic vision or Asmodeus *(detail)*. *Prado, Madrid. These two flying figures fill the left-hand half of the composition. One of them could represent Asmodeus, the devil mentioned in the Book of Tobit (Apocrypha). In an inventory drawn up in 1828 after Goya's death, where this work is mentioned for the first time, it is called "Asmodea", possibly because the figures were considered female, as can be observed in a curious sketch kept in the Museum in Basel. Apart from the question of whether one of them is a male or female devil, the fact is that the two figures give the scene a highly dramatic touch; there is something vaguely Michaelangelesque about them, resembling those floating in the first scenes of the Genesis in the Sistine Chapel.*

"scheme" we must limit it to the way in which the different compositions were distributed in the two rooms.

The ground floor room was presumably dominated by two large-scale works (over 4 metres wide by 1½ metres high) which probably covered one of the long walls. These would have been *The Witches' Sabbath* and *The Pilgrimage to St. Isidore's Hermitage*. The former depicts a throng of witches, with a he-goat on one side and a lady wearing a mantilla on the other, forming a mass of bodies with horribly deformed heads turned towards the animal in monk's attire that personifies the devil. In the other scene the figures in the group on its way to the saint's hermitage have grotesque faces that seem to cry out rather than sing to the guitar; there are also some cloaked figures, two men fighting and various other groups on different planes that in no way resemble the scene of *St. Isidore's Meadow*. The gay composition that Goya painted some 35 years earlier has now turned into a nightmarish spectacle that rings with the plaintive cries of the pilgrims. The four remaining murals in this room were most probably *Judith and Holofernes*, *Saturn devouring one of his sons*, a black-veiled lady who could be *Leocadia Zorrilla-Weiss* and *An old man and a monk*, where Xavier de Salas be-

Judith and Holofernes. Prado, Madrid. As in the other works, it should be remembered that there was once a landscape under this composition, inspite of its vertical shape. It was painted on one of the walls of the ground-floor room in Goya's country house on the other side of an open space from Saturn *devouring one of his sons, with which it should probably be related. The figure of Judith poised to kill Holofernes is dramatically forceful.*

lieved that he had discovered a suggestion of a self-portrait.

The eight paintings in the upper-floor room are not so easy to distribute logically. Even the interpretation of the subject-matter is an open question. It is too complex a matter to go into in detail here. Several of the pictures have two or even three titles; the varying sizes further complicate the question. The fact that this room was probably used as a dining-room is another aspect to be taken into consideration; it might account for one of the themes: *Two old people eating*, one of them apparently a witch with a spoon. *Reading* is the title (in the Prado Catalogue) of a composition which shows several figures looking at a paper apparently lying on the lap of the man in the centre.

186

187

Two old people eating. *Prado, Madrid. It is difficult to construe a hidden meaning in this work beyond what the eye sees. In the 1828 inventory it was named* Two witches. *Whoever the figures may be, its outstanding feature is its stark Expressionism. X-rays revealed alterations in the composition and once again signs of re-painting.*

Saturn devouring one of his sons. *Prado, Madrid. Its starkly realistic air popularized this work. The Roman god of Time, with gaping eyes, his hands convulsively clutching the boy's blood-stained, headless body, is a deeply moving image. Goya had probably seen the same subject depicted by Rubens, but rendered it here in his own forceful manner.*

Although it also has a symbolic meaning, the *Two women laughing with a man* appears to be a realistic sketch. The *Two men fighting with clubs* is stranger: one of them blood-stained, the men stand knee-deep in a quagmire against a background of lighter-coloured clouds. But the most enigmatic of these small-scale works is the *Head of a dog* that seems to emerge from the ground (?) looking attentively upwards; the question mark is justified because if the dog's head were not there this would be a non-figurative study in sienna tones.

The three most elaborate works are also the most difficult to identify as far as subject-matter is concerned. One is entitled *Pilgrimage to St. Isidore's well* in the Prado Catalogue and *The Holy Office* in the inventory that Goya's friend, the painter Antonio Brugada, drew up. The truth is that an outdoor scene like this, with mountains and trees in the background, does not appear to have much to do with the Inquisition; only a figure dressed in the costume of Philip IV's time, with a ruff, seems somewhat out of place. In general these various groups on different planes give the impression of a genre picture, as if it were an expressionistic version of a tapestry design. The other two paintings do not belong to the realm of reality because the principal figures are depicted flying through the air. The

The Witches' Sabbath (Aquelarre). The Pilgrimage to St. Isidore's hermitage. *Prado, Madrid. These two wide paintings probably faced one another from opposite ends of the lower room in the "Quinta". In the first one we have an impressing assembly of witches around the figure of "the great he-goat" and on the far side an attractive young spectator*

*with her hands in a muff, all of it
depicted in a vigorously
expressionistic manner. The other
work reveals the same technique and
visionary atmosphere in a scene
crammed with strange beings on
different planes that has nothing to do
with the gay* St. Isidore's Meadow
*that Goya painted some 30 years
earlier.*

Half-submerged dog. *Prado, Madrid. Without doubt this is the most puzzling of all these so-called "Black Paintings". The work was fundamentally a landscape, but even X-rays have revealed nothing to accompany the dog's head.*

first has a wealth of tonalities and strongly contrasted masses; it is called *Asmodeus* because it is believed to represent the so-named devil mentioned in the Book of Tobit. This interpretation, however, does not account for the men aiming their guns at the flying figures nor the other groups in the lower part of the picture, which rather seem to recall scenes of guerrilla warfare from the time of the Napoleonic occupation. The two figures in the air have something Michelangelesque about them. Finally we should mention the work that the painter and art theorist Aureliano de Beruete identified as *The Fates* and the Prado Catalogue simply calls *Fate*. It shows four figures floating in the air over an extensive landscape with trees; the

one seen full-face is a man, while the other three are vaguely female figures bearing a tiny effigy, a lens and a pair of scissors, symbolizing birth, transit through life and death.

Despite all the studies and conjectures, these paintings continue to be an enigma, also after laboratory tests were carried out in the Prado and the findings published by Carmen Garrido in 1984. X-rays revealed surprising alterations in various scenes. According to this, "bright clear landscapes with light-coloured clouds were possibly what Goya originally painted on these walls... Human figures were irrelevant in these land and skyscapes; only a few small ones appear in the lower parts". On top of these original landscapes Goya added the figures later (with the exception, for example, of *The Witches' Sabbath*), re-arranging the compositions, re-painting them, etc. Laboratory analyses of the pigments led to a better knowledge of the kind of paints Goya used and also revealed the delicate state of the paintings.

The Black Paintings deserve a special mention because in them Goya's technique can be seen at its boldest and because here he delves further than in any other series of his works into the infrahuman world of nightmarish creatures and disturbing symbols. These paintings prefigure contemporary Expressionism in the same way that the frescoes of San Antonio de la Florida or *The Executions of May 3rd* herald the beginnings of Impressionism. In spite of their wealth of chromatic values, they are indeed "black paintings", born in the subconscious of a man well into his seventies. As such they illustrate an important trend of present-day art, literature and thought.

DRAWINGS AND ETCHINGS

Reference has repeatedly been made in the preceding chapters to Goya's activity as a draughtsman and etcher. His artistic personality in these two fields is also extremely interesting because his spontaneity and sincerity are even greater here than in his paintings. And his output is also exceptional, especially in comparison with the very scarce production of drawings and etchings by other Spanish master painters. Ribera and Alonso Cano are exceptions in this respect in the 17th century. Goya began to work in these fields when he was about 30 and continued until the very end of his life. It is obvious that his technique and subjects changed substantially in these fifty years. On the other hand, if we put his drawings and etchings in chronological order we will find that he turned to these forms of expression at very irregular intervals, usually coinciding with periods of crisis in his life, sometimes due to ill health.

One aspect of Goya's work as a draughtsman is surprising and has given rise to an excellent study by Pierre Gassier. Among all these drawings it is difficult to find any preparatory studies for his paintings, as other artists have left. For Goya drawing was an independent activity and very often led to engraving, in the same way as a preliminary sketch is the first step towards an oil or fresco painting. Apart from this he also occasionally jotted down rapid notes of other artists' ideas which he later developed in elaborate compositions of his own.

The first definite news we have of Goya as an engraver dates from December 1778, following one of his spells of ill health. He is known to have engraved a series of prints after works by Velázquez, which reveals his great interest in Philip IV's Court Painter. Sánchez Cantón rightly emphasized the importance of Goya's discovery of Velázquez, whose influence often made itself felt in his art. Copying these eighteen paintings by the great master helped him to develop technical skills; his own inventiveness was to come later.

After recovering from his serious, almost fatal illness in 1792 and 1793, he once again turned to his drawing block and copper plates. A perfectly coherent line can be traced linking the strange disease that caused his deafness, his friendship with the Duchess of Alba and the "Sanlúcar Album", the sketchbook he filled during his stay at the Duchess' Andalusian estate. The result of his work as a draughtsman and engraver during these years was the famous series known as *Los Caprichos*. These etchings were completed by 1797, but they were not made public until two years later: a receipt dated January 17th 1799 records that they were sold to the Duchess of Osuna for 1500 *reales*.

An advertisement in the newspaper *Diario de Madrid* in February explained the *Caprichos* as follows: "Convinced as he is that censure of human errors and vices... can also be subject-matter for painting, the artist has chosen as fitting for his work from among the many follies and blunders common to every civil society, as well as from the vulgar

The Duchess of Alba in mourning. *Prado, Madrid. Indian ink wash drawing. It is one of the drawings that Sánchez Cantón grouped together in the so-called Sanlúcar sketchbooks that contain scenes that Goya made a note of during his stay in the Coto de Doñana with Cayetana de Alba. We agree with Lafuente Ferrari in assuming that this lady looking towards Goya and the viewer is the Duchess herself. The drawing was not used as an etching in the* Caprichos.

prejudices and lies accepted by custom, ignorance and egoism, those which he considers most suitable to be ridiculed and at the same time to exercise the artist's imagination". These words make the intention of the 80 etchings clear. After initial difficulties, including trouble with the Inquisition, in the long run this series achieved popularity and contributed decisively towards establishing Goya's fame beyond the frontiers of his own country.

Art critics such as Sánchez Cantón, López Rey, Lafuente Ferrari and Edith Helman analysed the subjects to be found in the *Caprichos* and attempted to explore Goya's mind which, without being that of a philosopher or a moralist, had visualized such an imaginative, satirical world in these drawings. Let us call to mind the famous print that was

Lineage. *Etching no. 57 of the* Caprichos. Caricatured mask. *Pen and ink drawing. Prado, Madrid. Side by side an etching and its preparatory studies offer an interesting opportunity to compare. Art historian Gassier accounts for at least three preliminary sketches for this etching; one in the so-called "Madrid Album" in the Louvre bears the title* Listed as a hermaphrodite; *the one reproduced here stresses the grotesque features, including the figure with a monocle who has a monkey on his shoulders, the woman wearing an ass-like mask and the individual with an outsize nose reading. The third, simplified version coincides with the etching.*

intended to provide the frontispiece of the series and in the end figured as no. 43 with the motto *"The dream of reason brings forth monsters"*. If we ignore the various different versions that Goya made in preparatory studies, we are left with the picture of the artist slumped face down on his desk, surrounded by owls, bats and other animals. An earlier design also included human faces hovering in the air. In the lower part, on the desk front, Goya added: "Universal language, drawn and engraved by Francisco de Goya. 1797... The artist dreaming: his intention is only to put an end to prejudicial

common practices and spread by means of these *Caprichos* the sound testimony of truth".

This is the plate that attained greatest renown, but we should not overlook the many others that overflow with satirical and fantastic touches, where rational beings give way to asses, witches hold gatherings with repelling outlandish creatures, an ugly old woman tries in vain to appear coquettish, while others amount to anti-clerical satires. Some scenes are of a more agreeable nature (including several that seem to represent the Duchess of Alba) and afford a respite from

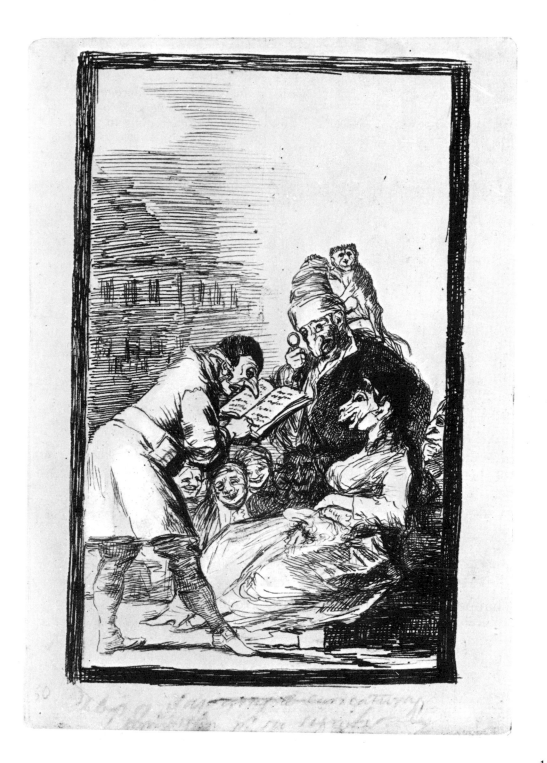

those that tend towards obscene subjects. Here Goya's genius reveals itself in his astonishing ability to make the most of caricature.

The second major series of drawings and engravings is the cycle already mentioned in an earlier chapter entitled *The Disasters of War*, whose subject-matter needs no further description. They were made between 1810 and 1820 and comprise a total of 82 plates.

The bullfight illustrations known as *La Tauromaquia* were the outcome of a more complicated process that was superbly studied by Lafuente Ferrari. They consist of 40 plates and were put up for sale in 1816. Here Goya reproduced surprisingly vigorous, varied and dramatic scenes of the popular *fiesta de toros*, including different kinds of passes by bullfighters on foot and on horseback, interpreted in red pencil with an extremely vibrating sense of movement and loose technique.

As in the case of the *Caprichos*, this collection of engravings was advertised in the *Diario de Madrid* on October 28th 1816 in the following terms: "Copper-plate etchings representing different stages of a bullfight... that illustrate the beginnings, development and present-day situation of the *fiesta* in Spain and require no further explanation". Indeed, the monographic subject-matter of *La*

200

The beds of death. Preparatory sketch for etching no. 62 of The Disasters of War *and the etching. Prado, Madrid. This sanguine sketch and the etching belong to a group known as "Emphatic caprices" within the* Disasters of War, *i.e. they are reminiscences of Goya's first set of etchings, the* Caprichos. *This one shows corpses bunched together awaiting burial. As Gassier pointed out, "drawing and etching should be examined side by side in order to appreciate how the aquatint process enabled Goya to re-distribute light and shade over the copper-plate to obtain effects that the sanguine alone could only render vaguely. In this scene the lighting produces a special contrast between the almost black background and the luminous figure of the hooded woman, while behind her formless shapes of bodies cover the ground: an image of desolation and death as befits the title of the etching".*

Tauromaquia makes this the most consistent of Goya's series of engravings.

The last set of etchings is one that the Academy published in 1863 with the title *The Proverbs*, but which is now more commonly known as *Los Disparates* (*disparate*, meaning something absurd or nonsensical, being the word that Goya used in a large number of the captions). These include 18 plates, as well as four other unpublished etchings that were brought to public notice by the magazine *L'Art*. Executed about the same time as the Black Paintings, they are similar, if not in subject-matter, at least in atmosphere. Their original captions are sufficiently significant: *Feminine absurdity, Fearful absurdity, Ridiculous absurdity, Flying absurdity, Furious absurdity, Absurdity of marriage, General absurdity, Poor absurdity, Evident absurdity* and many others titles of scenes depicted in an overwhelmingly imaginative vein.

Goya's bent for drawing and engraving remained with him until the very end. In 1825 he wrote to his friend Ferrer commenting on new editions. He also made some lithographs with animal subjects, which confirm that he was not at his best drawing animals; however, about the same time he executed the set known as *The Bulls of Bor-*

The way in which the ancient Spaniards used to capture bulls on horseback in the open country. Pepe Illo dodging the bull.
Preparatory sketches in sanguine for etchings nos. 1 and 29 of La Tauromaquia (Art of bullfighting). Prado, Madrid. This set of engravings was offered for sale at the end of 1816, three of them having been etched already a year before. Goya prepared them therefore after the war and their subject-matter above suspicion permitted him to announce them for sale immediately. He used a historical approach, depicting bullfighting in the Middle Ages, with scenes of Moors trying their skill, the Cid spearing a bull, etc. The preparatory drawing for the first etching shows a picador *energetically goading a bull. However, in the finished engraving this scene is treated more conventionally and the figure has been altered. The sketch for etching no. 29 was the first of a number of drawings that Goya made of the famous Sevillian bullfighter José Delgado Gálvez, known as Pepe Illo, who died in the bullring in Madrid in 1801 at the age of 47. In this scene he has just carried out a dangerous move near the bull's horns. Observe Goya's skill at reproducing with a minimum of lines the whole scene in the bullring as well as some of the spectators.*

203

A bad dream. *Lithographic pencil drawing. Prado, Madrid. In his old age in Bordeaux Goya revived subjects that had obsessed him in the past. This drawing with birds pecking at a terrified face belongs to the so-called* Caprichos nuevos. *A startled man accompanied by two cats observes the vision.*

Gran disparate

Great absurdity. *Soft lithographic pencil drawing. Prado, Madrid. In spite of its title (in Spanish, Gran disparate), this drawing was not etched for the series of the Disparates or Proverbs as they were originally called. It belongs to another set made in Bordeaux in 1825, but never etched. It is sufficiently expressive to need no further commentary and demonstrates how Goya's extraordinary imagination continued to work at the age of almost 80.*

deaux consisting of four very original and lively etchings.

It is an open question whether the last drawing that Goya completed before his death was the one depicting a very old man leaning on two sticks that bears the caption "I am still learning", but Sánchez Cantón rightly remarked that this could indeed be a fitting motto to sum up his long and fruitful life.

CHRONICLE OF GOYA'S LIFE

The following biographical facts are based for the most part on documented evidence, in particular Goya's letters to Martín Zapater.

1746 Goya was born on March 30th in the village of Fuendetodos (province of Saragossa), the son of José Goya, a gilder, and Gracia née Lucientes, whose family belonged to the lower gentry. His parents had married in 1736. The reason why they were in Fuendetodos at the time of Goya's birth is unknown, as well as the date of their return to Saragossa.

1760 Goya was training in the workshop of José Luzán Martínez in Saragossa.

1763 On December 4th he was in Madrid to participate in a competition held at the Royal Academy of Fine Arts of San Fernando to grant scholarships to young artists to study in Rome.

1764 In the examination held on January 15th, in which he was required to make a pencil sketch of a statue of "Silenus", he did not obtain a single vote.

1766 In this year's examination the subject set for the "prepared" test on January 5th was "The Empress Martha of Constantinople appearing before King Alfonso the Wise at Burgos to ask him for a third of the ransom price due to the Sultan of Egypt for her husband the Emperor Baldwin's liberty (and the King granted her the whole sum)". For the "impromptu" test held on January 22nd the chosen subject was: "Juan de Urbina and Diego de Paredes discussing before the Spanish army in Italy which of the two should be given the arms of the Marquis of Pescara". The first prize was won by Ramón Bayeu, who was later to become Goya's brother-in-law, and Goya again did not obtain a single vote.

1767 Goya probably painted two pictures entitled, according to Charles Yriarte, *The proclamation of the order expelling the Jesuits* and *The enforcement of the order expelling the Jesuits.*

1771 On April 20th Goya wrote to notify the Academy of Parma that he had dispatched a painting of *Hannibal crossing the Alps* as set on May 20th of the previous year for a competition. On this occasion Goya was awarded six votes when the results were published on June 27 th.

1772 Between January and July several payments are recorded as having been paid to Goya by the chapter in Saragossa for the fresco he was painting in the cupola of the Holy Chapel (in the Basilica of Our Lady of the Pillar). It had been commissioned on October 21st of the previous year, which implies that Goya had returned from Italy prior to that date.

1773 On July 25th Francisco Goya and María Josefa Bayeu were married at St. Mary's church in Madrid.

1774 When Mengs returned to Italy, Goya probably received his first commission to paint cartoons for the Royal Tapestry Manufactory.

1775 Goya submitted a number of hunting and fishing scenes to the Royal Tapestry Manufactory on different dates during this year. On November 6th he wrote to his friend Martín Zapater: "Here I have a St. Christopher and on the other side I'll paint you a Sorrowing Virgin..."

1776 On October 30th Goya informed Sabatini that he had painted "a picnic scene" for the Royal Tapestry Manufactory. This same year Mengs referred in a letter to what he believed the artists José del Castillo, Ramón Bayeu and Goya should be paid for their work for the Tapestry Manufactory. He thought José del Castillo was worth 9000 *reales* and the others 8000 "for the time being". Goya was considered "a talented individual who is expected to make good progress in art".

1777 On January 22nd Goya wrote to Zapater: "It looks as though my wife is going to give birth today". In this year there are references to a painting of a "dance on the banks of the Manzanares" delivered to the Royal Tapestry Manufactory and to several other commissions. In March Goya wrote to Zapater: "I am up but

feeling so bad that I don't know where my head is; I'm off my food and everything else". On April 16th he wrote again: "I'm well again, thank God that I got over it". In another letter, written presumably about the same time, he remarked: "I'm off to the opera and by God I am sorry that you cannot attend these entertainments with me".

1778 On April 27th reference is made to a painting "to be copied in a tapestry" depicting a scene in the Plaza de la Cebada, a lively market place, with a blind man singing to his guitar in the foreground and his guide boy standing next to him... This picture was returned "to be corrected". In July and December several prints are mentioned "drawn and etched by Don Francisco Goya... after life-size originals by Don Diego Velázquez in the Royal Palace collection". Goya referred to several bullfighting scenes in a letter to Zapater on October 7th.

1779 On January 9th Goya wrote Zapater, among other news, "if I had more time I would tell you how the King and the Crown Prince and Princess have honoured me: I showed them four of my pictures and kissed their hands; it was the first time I had the honour to do so and I assure you I could not wish for more than for my work to please them, which it did and the King and even more their Royal Highnesses were very satisfied with me". In February six of Goya's paintings for the Royal Tapestry Manufactory were valued at 20 000 *reales*. On August 6th he applied for a post as Court Painter. On this occasion Mengs' judgement three years earlier was recalled: "He is a hard-working artist, talented and spirited... who can continue to do paintings for the Tapestry Manufactory, taking pains to develop his skill and progress...". On November 25th Goya received 15 015 *reales* as an advance payment from the chapter in Saragossa for frescoes in one of the cupolas of the Virgin of the Pillar basilica.

1780 A document dated January 24th contains an "inventory of the paintings being delivered by Don Francisco Goya". On May 5th he applied to become a Fellow of the Royal Academy of Fine Arts of San Fernando "presenting for this reason an original work depicting Our Lord Crucified". In his correspondence with Zapater during this year he referred to his satisfactory economic situation; in July he remarked: "For my home I do not need much furniture; it seems to me that so long as there is an image of Our Lady of the Pillar, a table, five chairs, a frying pan, a wineskin, a small guitar, a roasting jack and candles, everything else is unnecessary". On August 23rd he informed his friend: "Pepa has brought forth a very pretty boy, thank God". During this year frequent references are made to commissions for the basilica in Saragossa.

1781 On March 17th Goya sent a long report to the Basilica building committee, entitling himself an Academician of San Fernando and giving vent to his anger over criticism of his painting for the cupola and the necessity of submitting it to his brother-in-law Francisco Bayeu's judgement. After several exchanges of letters he finally agreed to carry out new sketches. On July 25th he

enthusiastically informed Zapater that he had been chosen to contribute a painting to the decoration of the church of San Francisco el Grande in Madrid. He referred to details of this work in a number of letters (especially in one addressed to the Count of Floridablanca). His correspondence during this year also contains frequent references to his family and particularly his father's ill-health.

1782 In his letters to Zapater Goya commented on various aspects of his daily life, such as economic affairs, purchases of clothing, receiving foodstuffs and matters of health, particularly regarding Josefa's weakness after a miscarriage. An inventory signed by Cornelius van der Goten and dated January 17th indicates which of Goya's works had been delivered to the Tapestry Manufactory by this date.

1783 Possibly the most important events of this year are connected with Goya's stay at the Infante Don Luis' palace in Arenas de San Pedro. On September 20th he wrote to Zapater: "His Highness has showered me with honours; I have done his portrait and also that of his wife and son and daughter and received unexpected praise because other painters have attempted to do the same unsuccessfully. I have been out shooting with His Highness twice and he is a good shot; the other day he said as we were discussing shooting a rabbit "this dauber here is still more of an enthusiast than I am". I have been with these people for a whole month and they are goodness itself. They have given me a thousand *duros* and a gown for my wife, all embroidered in silver and gold, the wardrobe keepers there say it is worth 30 000 *reales*. And they were so sorry to see me leave that they could not get over it". In his correspondence (apart from a remark about the Crown Prince criticizing one of Bayeu's paintings) Goya also referred to the fact that the Count of Floridablanca had commissioned him to paint his portrait. As well as some domestic affairs, the letters also reveal that the paintings for the San Francisco el Grande church had already been hung.

1784 Goya's letters to Zapater continue to contain interesting news about his domestic situation (he was "extremely tired" of helping his family in Saragossa out financially), about the pictures he was painting for the Infante Don Luis (which enabled him to take part in more shooting parties in Arenas de San Pedro) and some re-painting of his work in San Francisco el Grande. On December 4th he announced the birth two days earlier of yet another son, Francisco Javier, remarking: "May God let this one survive". His wish was heard. A reference to the portrait he had painted of the Count of Floridablanca reveals how little the work met with the eminent politician's approval. On October 11th Jovellanos wrote to Goya expressing his satisfaction over the four works (unfortunately now lost) that he had painted for the Calatrava College of Salamanca University.

1785 On May 4th Goya informed Zapater confidentially but jubilantly that his name had been put forward for the post of Deputy Director of Painting at the Royal Academy of San Fernando. Other letters reflect his interest in hunting and shooting. In

another he described the visit that the King, Crown Prince and Princess and Infantes paid to the Virgin of Atocha church: "there was very good lighting and the Plaza Mayor looked at its best". He also commented on the Infante Don Luis' bad health (he did indeed die soon afterwards). Important commissions this year included portraits for the Bank of San Carlos, as well as of the Duke and Duchess of Osuna and Duke and Duchess of Medinaceli.

1786 On July 7th Goya wrote Zapater: "Now I am one of the King's Painters with a salary of 15 000 *reales*". A few days later he related how he had fallen while trying out a new carriage or gig. This letter reflects his comfortable economic position and reputation and also contains interesting remarks about his works for the Royal Tapestry Manufactory as well as *costumbrista* scenes for the Osuna palace. In December he wrote his friend to thank him for sending him twelve bars of *turrón*, a typical Christmas sweet...

1787 Goya's letters during this year contain good-humoured references to his economic well-being, hunting, various family affairs and show that it was a successful year for him, including visits to the Alameda de Osuna palace, not only to paint but also to go riding. He replaced his two-wheeled gig by a four-wheeled carriage. In May however he remarked that his wife was ill "and the boy still worse", although both recovered later. As far as his work is concerned, apart from the paintings for the Alameda de Osuna and the Tapestry Manufactory, he did three canvases for St. Anne's in Valladolid. His correspondence reflects an optimistic mood, although on November 28th he wrote Zapater: "I have turned old, with so many wrinkles you would not recognize me except for my flat nose and sunken eyes... I must say, I am very much feeling my 41 years...".

1788 Goya continued to work actively for the Tapestry Manufactory, the San Carlos bank and the Alameda de Osuna palace; he also painted the large-scale pictures that the Duke of Osuna had commissioned for the Cathedral in Valencia. On March 19th he wrote a letter of recommendation to his friend Zapater for one "Paco Trigo, of Madrid, famous as a singer and guitar-player; he astonished the people of Cadiz and also here in Madrid and I hope he will do the same there: I would appreciate it if you take an interest in him and help him to sing wherever you see fit...".

1789 As a result of Charles III's death on December 14th of the previous year, work at the Royal Tapestry Manufactory was interrupted. On April 25th the new monarch Charles IV appointed Goya Court Painter "with the same privileges that he has enjoyed until now". Together with other painters he was charged with "inspecting and assessing the late King's works of art". In his correspondence with Zapater Goya again mentioned that he was having to help his family in Saragossa financially, which was becoming more and more of a burden to him, especially his sister Rita.

Among the works he completed this year were a number of royal portraits for the Palace and the Academy of History.

1790 This year Goya painted a picture that the King had commissioned for his brother the King of Naples, as well as more tapestry cartoons. On August 28th he wrote to Zapter: "I am in Valencia; I came with my wife for the sea air over a fortnight ago". In October he was made an honorary member of the Fine Arts Academy of San Carlos in Valencia. The same month he was also appointed an honorary member of the Royal Society of Friends of Aragon. He was in Saragossa at the time, having improvised a visit there with a friend. Although he was unwell in December, he ended the year optimistically and in a good mood, to judge by the jovial tone of his letters.

1791 Goya worked on tapestry cartoons again and was required to assess the paintings in the new Royal Palace. In December he wrote Zapater: "Today I have been to see the King and he was glad to see me. He asked me about my Paco's pox (which he already knew about), I told him, he pressed my hand and then started to play the violin. I was afraid to go and see him because some members of my profession had told him in that same room that I did not want to serve him and other things that wretched men do...".

1792 Goya submitted a list of expenses incurred in painting cartoons for tapestries intended for the palace at El Escorial. On October 14th, having been asked his opinion about the classes at the Royal Academy, he replied with a long commentary on the subject, in which he pointed out, among other things, that "Art Academies should not be exclusive, nor should they be more than a help for those who choose to study in them freely, discarding notions like compulsory attendance, fixed principles, monthly prizes and other petty things that debase and undermine such a liberal and noble art as painting". At some unknown date after writing this memorandum Goya must have left for Andalusia, where he fell seriously ill. In the Archives of the Royal Academy of San Fernando there is a note that reads: "Goya has been absent since October '92; he only attended the General Assembly on July 11th '93, but not the other meetings that year" (Acad. Arch. 1-14/5). The portrait he painted of his friend Sebastián Martínez, with whom he stayed in Cadiz, is dated 1792. (Four years later he painted three semi-circular pictures for the Holy Grotto church there).

1793 In January the Duke of Frias informed that "Don Francisco Goya has been granted two months' leave of absence to convalesce in Andalusia". On the 17th Goya requested Manuel de Cubas "to do me the favour of informing His Excellency that I have been in bed with colics for two months; I have leave of absence to travel to Seville and Cadiz and I beg His Excellency to give instructions that I may be supplied with money in Seville...". It appears that Goya left Madrid without permission and obtained it subsequently when he was already ill in Andalusia. On January 19th Zapater wrote to Sebastián Martínez: "Your esteemed letter of the 5th of this month has caused me the same anxiety about our dear Goya as your first letter and since the nature of his illness is of the most fearful, I am heavy-hearted about his possibilities of recovery... I am convinced of the exquisite hospitality that you are giving him and the affection that he is receiving from your family to help and console him in such a critical situation...". On March 19th Sebastián Martínez wrote to Pedro Arascot from Cadiz: "My friend Francisco de Goya departed from Madrid, as Your Worship is aware, in order to visit this and other cities on the way during his two months' leave of absence; however, he fell ill in Seville and, believing that he would be better looked after here, decided to be brought here by a friend. He entered my house in a very poor state and continues so, without having been able to leave the house since then. Everything has to be done to achieve his recovery, but I fear it will be a long process...". Ten days later Sebastián Martínez informed Zapater: "Our friend Goya is getting on slowly, but slightly improved. I trust that the coming season and the waters of Trillo, when he is able to take them, will help him to recover. The noises in his head and his deafness remain the same, but his sight is better and he is not as confused as he was, which made him lose his balance. He can walk up and down stairs now and do other things that he was unable to do...". A letter from Zapater to Francisco Bayeu is dated a day later, March 30th: "Goya's lack of self-concern has brought this on him but now he must be regarded with the compassion that his misfortune demands; he is a sick man, for whom everything must be done to ease his suffering, as you have done, obtaining leave of absence for his convalescence". Despite his illness there are documents pertaining to works he had carried out. On February 9th he

212

signed a receipt "in Saragossa" (sic) for "four transparencies for the Assembly Hall" and "two allegorical paintings of Saragossa", probably done the previous year for the City Council. On June 30th he wrote to the Royal Tapestry Manufactory submitting an account for the purchase of "colours" and requesting a rise due to the death of Ramón Bayeu.

1794 On January 4th Goya wrote to the Vice-Protector of the Academy, Bernardo de Iriarte, in the following terms: "Sir, in order to occupy my imagination mortified by my ill-health and to compensate part of the considerable expenses derived from the same, I have painted a set of cabinet pictures which allowed me to make observations that cannot normally be expressed in commissioned works, which offer no scope for flights of fancy or inventiveness. I am considering sending them to the Academy for the purposes you know and I can promise to submit the works to the approval of the members, but as a safeguard I have seen fit to send your Lordship these pictures first, due to the respect with which they will be viewed by your Lordship, whose authority and special intelligence cannot be sufficiently praised. I beg your Lordship to protect them and also to protect me in this situation in which I am more than ever in need of your kindly patronage...". Goya referred to the same matter again in other letters to the same personality. In letters to Zapater he alluded to his deafness, to a camp bed and to domestic affairs. At the Tapestry Manufactory an entry dated April 18th noted that "since Ramón Bayeu's death

Goya has not delivered a single work and apparently he is completely prevented from painting as a result of an accident". On April 25th Francisco Bayeu and Mariano Maella informed the Tapestry Manufactory that "although it is true that Francisco de Goya has undergone a serious illness, it is equally true that he has partly recovered and is painting again, although not as assiduously as before...

1795 On August 4th Francisco Bayeu died. A letter to Zapater that Goya playfully dated "London, August 2nd 1800" must have been written after Bayeu's death. In it he wrote, among other things: "You would do better to come and help me paint the lady of Alba who let herself into my studio yesterday to have me paint her face, in which she succeeded; incidentally, it appeals to me more than painting on canvas. I also have to paint her full-length and she will come as soon as I have finished a preliminary sketch I am doing of the Duke of Alcudia on horseback..." Further on he remarked about this picture of Godoy (Duke of Alcudia since 1792): "Bayeu should have done it, but he absconded...". Since the full-length portrait dedicated to the Duchess of Alba in the Liria Palace is dated 1795, the letter presumably has to be dated in the last five months of that year, although the commentaries of Beroqui and Salas-Agueda, who believe it was written in 1794, also deserve to be taken into account. After Bayeu's death Goya applied for the post of Director of the Royal Academy, assuring that he was "in a position to attend the Sketching Room during the months required and correct

213

the students' drawings". On September 13th he was indeed appointed to the post. His salary as Court Painter during this year is registered as 15 000 *reales*.

1796 On June 9th the Duke of Alba died in Seville and his widow retired to her palace in the Coto de Doñana, near Sanlúcar de Barrameda, to pass the time of mourning. At the end of this year or early in the following one Goya travelled to Andalusia again, where he painted the semi-circular paintings for the Holy Grotto in Cadiz and visited the Duchess of Alba in Doñana.

1797 Goya painted the portrait of the Duchess wearing a mantilla in the Coto de Doñana. On April 1st he wrote to the Academy relinquishing the post of Director due to bad health. In this letter he claimed that his "ailments, instead of diminishing, have become worse". In reply "the Academy, while admitting that the reason is just, true and sincere, very much regrets the distressing state of the distinguished artist's health and that one of his ailments should be such a severe deafness that he hears nothing at all, a circumstance that would prevent his students from posing questions during his art lessons". It was therefore proposed that Goya be relieved of his duties and included among the Academy's honorary directors, as was thus agreed. Apart from several paintings, during this year Goya must also have carried out a large number of drawings and etchings for *Los Caprichos*.

1798 Goya submitted a bill to the Duke of Osuna for "six composition pictures of witchcraft which are in the Alameda palace". Furthermore Leandro Fernández de Moratín mentioned in his "Diary" having seen the paintings in San Antonio de la Florida on May 21st; a report dated in December refers to "paints and the like" delivered to Goya for his work in this chapel. Some important portraits such as those of *General Urrutia*, *Guillemardet* and *Jovellanos* date from this year.

1799 In April the Duchess of Alba ordered payment to be made to Goya for "seven paintings representing, one, *St. Isidore's Meadow*, four of them, *The Seasons of the Year* and two others, country scenes". In Queen Maria Luisa's letters to Godoy there are references to various portraits by Goya, including an equestrian one. Together with Maella Goya was appointed Principal Court Painter with a salary of 50 000 *reales*. On Octuber 3rd he wrote the last datable letter to Zapater, in which he commented: "The King and Queen are crazy about your friend". Publication was announced of a "collection of fanciful scenes devised and etched by Don Francisco de Goya. Convinced as he is that censuring human errors and vices (which may seem to be the object of eloquence and poetry) can also be the aim of painting, the artist has chosen as appropriate subjects for his work from among the many follies and blunders common to every civil society, as well as from among the vulgar prejudices and lies accepted by custom, ignorance or selfishness, those which he considers most suitable to be held up to ridicule and at the same time to inspire an artist's imagination..." (several more paragraphs follow and the text concludes) "For sale at number 1. Desengaño Street, in the liquor and perfume shop, at 320 *reales-vellón* each set of 80 illustrations".

1800 In reply to an order for both Maella and Goya to be employed in producing carpet designs, the latter declared that "since your servant's activity has only consisted in painting histories and figures and doubting that he would be able to do decorative designs, having never done so before, he begs Your Majesty to commission him to carry out such pictures and supervise the work of professional decorative artists". In her correspondence with Godoy Queen Maria Luisa mentioned the portrait that Goya was painting of Godoy's wife, the Countess of Chinchón, and others of herself and members of the royal family, including "one of all of us together here", that is, *The Family of Charles IV*.

1801 On July 1st Goya submitted an account of expenses pertaining to a series of royal portraits he had been working on during the year. On March 5th he declared to the mayor of Toledo, while assessing the value of various paintings, that the was "totally and absolutely deaf", entitling himself not only "First Court Painter", but also "Director of the Royal Academy of San Fernando".

1802 The 13th Duchess of Alba died. Her will, dated five years earlier in Sanlúcar de Barrameda, included a bequest of 10 *reales* daily on behalf of Goya's son.

1803 Goya offered the *Caprichos* etchings in writing to the King, explaining among other things: "They are very much sought after by foreign collectors and in order to avoid them falling into foreign hands after my death I wish to present them to my Lord and King for his collection of engravings. I do not ask His Majesty for anything other than a small recompense for my son Francisco Javier de Goya to enable him to travel; he is keen and would benefit from it...". The ultimate reason for this offer was probably fear of the Inquisition.

1804 The lack of documents is compensated by a number of portraits painted by Goya this year, e.g. *The Marquis of San Adrián*.

1805 On July 8th Goya's son Francisco Javier married Maria Gumersinda Goicoechea in the church of San Ginés. She was the daughter of Martín Miguel Goicoechea and Juana née Galarza. For this occasion Goya painted a set of miniature portraits of his son, Francisco Javier's parents-in-law and their daughters.

1806 Goya was paid for a portrait of the Academy Director, Vargas Ponce. On March 28th the King ordered that the sum of 12 000 *reales* yearly should continue to be paid to Francisco Javier Goya in compensation for *Los Caprichos*. On July 11th Pío Mariano, the son of Francisco Javier Goya, was baptized. Goya donated his house in the Calle de los Reyes to his son.

1807 In a letter to Fray Manuel Bayeu, Jovellanos wrote: "Since you make no mention of Sr. Goya, we are led to doubt that he travelled to Saragossa as intended; but if, on the contrary, he is there, please do not forget to greet him on behalf of this friend who always remembers him with great affection". Goya continued to paint portraits.

1808 When Ferdinand VII ascended the throne as a result of the uprising in Aranjuez on March 19th, the Royal Academy of San Fernando considered that "it appears urgent to paint a portrait of the new King". The council decided as mentioned in a document: "Be Don Francisco de Goya comissioned to carry it out". This resolution was passed on March 28th and the Academy's archives subsequently contain a number of documents pertaining to this portrait, which is the equestrian one kept in the Academy now. In 1814 it still had not been paid for and on October 14th 1816 reference was made anew to this payment in a curious memorandum, that also mentions the *Crucifixion* that had been passed on to San Francisco el Grande. On October 2nd 1808 Goya informed José Munárriz that "His Excellency Don José Palafox has called for me to go to Saragossa this week to see the ruins of the city in order to paint them, which I cannot turn down because the glory of my home city concerns me so much".

1809 In a letter to the Academician José Munárriz, dated May 5th, Goya wrote: "While I was absent from the capital I received Your Honour's message of November 8th... referring to the picture that I painted at your request". Apart from the mention of King Ferdinand's portrait, this letter confirms Goya's visit to Saragossa. On December 23rd the Madrid City Council commissioned Goya to paint an allegorical picture with a portrait of Joseph Bonaparte in a medallion.

1810 In addition to the above work for the Madrid City Council, which later underwent a number of transformations due to political circumstances, Goya must have completed many of the genre scenes and engravings for the *Disasters of War* series.

1811 On March 11th Goya swore allegiance to the King, Joseph Bonaparte. On June 3rd he made a will, together with his wife, designating their son Francisco Javier as sole heir. The "intruder king" awarded Goya the "Royal Order of Spain", disparagingly known as the "Aubergine Order" due to its colour.

1812 On June 20th Goya's wife Josefa died. For this reason an inventory of the artist's belongings was set up, in order to assign to the son and heir what was due to him; this inventory included a curious list of pictures. Goya painted Wellington's portrait this year. In this connection the writer Mesonero Romanos refers in an interesting passage to a violent argument between the painter and the famous English general. A public showing of the portrait was announced on September 1st in the Academy.

1813 There are no known documental references to Goya in this year apart from mentions of his allegorical work for the City of Madrid.

1814 On February 24th Goya wrote to the Regency Council expressing his "ardent desire to perpetuate by means of my paint-brush the most memorable and heroic episodes of our glorious uprising against the tyrant of Europe: considering my state of absolute penury and consequent incapacity to bear the cost of such an interesting work, I request assistance from the public treasury to carry it out". The Regency council granted Goya's petition on March 3rd. Various documents in June and July referred to a portrait of the king for the regional authorities of Navarra. In November, in a hearing about Goya's conduct during the war, several witnesses declared on his behalf.

1815 The commission judging political responsibilities decided to declare Goya in the so-called "first class category", i.e. free of guilt, thus justifying his conduct. On March 16th he was summoned to appear before the court of the Holy Office to declare whether he was the author of paintings considered obscene: the *Majas* are meant. During this year there are several documental references to portraits of the king by Goya.

1816 A "collection of etchings by Don Francisco de Goya, Court Painter, representing bullfights in our arenas" was put on sale. Several portraits are dated this year.

1817 Ceán Bermúdez wrote in a letter: "I am at present occupied in instilling into Goya a sense of decorum, modesty, devotion, respectful action, dignified and simple composition with religious feelings for a large-scale canvas commissioned by the Cathedral chapter in Seville... The martyrs St. Justa and St. Rufina are the subject-matter".

1818 On January 14th the above-mentioned painting was hung in the Cathedral in Seville.

1819 On February 27th Goya bought a house named "la Quinta del Sordo" (i.e. the Deaf Man's Villa) outside Madrid, near the Segovia bridge. In May he received a commission to paint a picture representing *The Last Communion of St. Joseph Cala-*

sanz for the San Antón schools. Another painting, dated 1820, bears the following text: "From Goya to his friend Arrieta in gratitude for the skill and attention with which he saved his life during his serious and dangerous illness at the end of 1819, at the age of 73..."

1820 The above-mentioned work contains the last self-portrait of Goya, being attended here by his physician, Dr. Arrieta. On April 8th Goya's presence is registered at the Royal Academy in a ceremony to swear allegiance to the Constitution.

1821-23 There are scarcely any documents concerning Goya during these years. He must have carried out the decoration of the "Quinta del Sordo" with the so-called "Black Paintings" around this time, or possibly earlier. When Ferdinand VII was re-instated as an absolutist monarch, Goya made over the "Quinta" to his grandson Mariano (September 17th 1823), probably to avoid having it confiscated.

1824 During the first quarter of this year Goya took refuge in the house of his friend Duaso to escape political reprisals. On May 2nd he requested the king for leave to travel to Plombières in France to take a thermal cure. Having obtained permission, he left for Bordeaux on May 30th. On June 27th Leandro Fernández de Moratín wrote to Juan Antonio Melón: "Goya arrived indeed, old, deaf, slow in movements and weak, knowing not a word of French and without even a servant (which he needs most of all), but content and eager to see the world. He spent three days here; he came to lunch with us twice as if he were a young student: I begged him to return here by September and not get bogged down in Paris because if winter surprises him there it would be the end of him...". Some curious documents reveal that he was discreetly spied on by the police during his stay in Paris. Thanks to Moratín we know that on September 29th Goya was back in Bordeaux and living with Leocadia Zorrilla. Moratín remarked: "I cannot observe the slightest harmony between them".

1825 On January 13th his leave of absence was extended by the king "in order to take a cure in Bagnères, which he hopes will restore his health". On April 14th Leandro Fernández de Moratín wrote to Juan Antonio Melón again: "Goya, at his 79 years of age and with his aches and pains, does not know what his hopes or his needs are: I plead with him to stay here quietly until his leave of absence expires. He enjoys the town and the countryside, the climate, the food, his independence and the peace he has here. Since he has been here he has not suffered from any of the complaints he had back there, but sometimes he gets it into his head that he has a lot to do in Madrid; and if he were allowed he would be off on a wretched mule, with his cap and cloak, his wooden stirrups, his wineskin and his saddle-bags...". On May 29th two doctors certified that Goya "is at present suffering from paralysis of the bladder". His complaint is described in detail, no doubt in order to send a report to Spain; however, the acuteness of his illness is confirmed in a letter from Moratín to Manuel García de la Parda: "He has been on the verge of death". On June 21st Francisco Javier requested that his father's leave of absence be extended for a further year, to which the king agreed.

1826 From Leandro Fernández de Moratín's correspondence we know that Goya was preparing to leave Bordeaux early in May: "He will be travelling alone and discontent with the French. If he is lucky and no harm befalls him on the way you will have every reason to congratulate him on his arrival and if he does not arrive, do not be surprised because the slightest indisposition could strike him down in the corner of some inn". On June 17th Goya was granted retirement "with his full salary of 50 000 *reales* as a pension... and also the King's leave to return to France..." In July Goya was back in Bordeaux.

1827 In a letter to Melón dated January 28th Moratín wrote: "I have not seen Goya for several days (the ice and snow have been terrible), but I do remember hearing them talk about some blankets that they received. It is strange that Doña Leocadia has not written you, but do not be surprised that Goya has not done so because he has great difficulty in writing a letter".

1828 Goya wrote to his son on January 17th in good spirits at the prospect of Javier's forthcoming visit to Bordeaux with his wife and son. Another letter on March 12th refers to Mariano and his mother's planned trip to Paris. On the 26th Goya wrote: "I am impatient awaiting my dear travellers (his daughter-in-law and grandson) and very anxious... I feel a lot better and hope to recover my health". In April he added a few lines to a letter that Mariano had written to his father; these are the last words in Goya's handwriting: "Dear Javier: All I can say is that such happiness has been a little too much for me and I am now in bed. May God allow me to see you come and fetch them so that my pleasure may be complete. Good-bye, your father Francisco". On April 16th the Spanish consul in Bordeaux certified: "...by virtue of verbal notification from Don Mariano de Goya concerning the death of his grandfather, Don Francisco de Goya y Lucientes, His Majesty's First Court Painter, which occurred at 2 a.m. on this day...".

BIBLIOGRAPHY

It is virtually impossible to list all the most relevant works published about Goya. As this book enters the press, the late Juan Antonio GAYA NUÑO's *Bibliografía crítica y antológica de Goya* has not yet been published; the proofs were at the Editora Nacional when this publishing house was closed down.

Although extremely useful in the past, Genaro ESTRADA's *Bibliografía de Goya* (Casa de España en México, 1940) and Agustín RUIZ CABRIADA's *Aportación a una bibliografía de Goya* (Biblioteca Nacional, Madrid, 1946) have in the meantime inevitably become outdated. The following list of works contains those referred to here in the text or notes, as well as some others that the reader might find of interest to enlarge on definite aspects touched on in this necessarily restricted survey of Goya's life and works. Some of the catalogues published for Goya exhibitions also include interesting essays that are worth consulting and have therefore been listed here.

ACHIARDI, Pierre D.: *Les Dessins de D. Francisco de Goya y Lucientes du Musée du Prado à Madrid.* Rome, 1908.

ADHEMAR, J.: *Goya.* Paris, 1941.

AGUEDA, Mercedes: *Novedades en torno a una serie de cartones de Goya.* "Boletín del Museo del Prado", n.º 13, 1984.

AGUILERA, Emilio: *Dibujos y grabados de Goya.* 3rd edition. Iberia, Barcelona, 1960.

ALCALA FLECHA, Roberto: *Matrimonio y prostitución en el arte de Goya.* Cáceres, 1984.

— *Literatura e ideología en el arte de Goya.* Saragossa, 1988.

ALVAREZ LOPERA, José: *De Goya, la Constitución y la prensa liberal.* In "Goya y la Constitución de 1812", pp. 29-52 of the Catalogue of the exhibition held in the Municipal Museum, Madrid, in December 1982-January 1983.

ANGELIS, Rita de: *L'opera pittorica completa di Goya.* Milan, 1974. (Spanish edition published in the collection "Clásicos del Arte". Ed. Noguer, S.A., Barcelona, 1976).

ANGULO IÑIGUEZ, Diego: *La familia del Infante Don Luis por Goya.* "Archivo Español de Arte", vol. XIV, 1940-41, p. 64.

— *El "Saturno" y las pinturas negras de Goya.* "Archivo Español de Arte", vol. XXX, n.º 138, pp. 173-7, 1962.

— *Un Goya y seis cuadros franceses a la Pinacoteca de Munich. El ejemplo del Banco Hipotecario de Baviera.* "Archivo Español de Arte", vol XXXIX, n.º 154-5, p. 271 and ff.

— *Murillo y Goya.* "Goya", n.º 148-50, 1979.

ARAUJO SANCHEZ, Ceferino: *Goya.* Madrid, 1896.

ARNAIZ, José Manuel and MONTERO, Angel: *Goya y el Infante Don Luis.* "Anticuaria", n.º 27, 1986, pp. 45-55.

BARRENO SEVILLANO, Luisa: *El retrato del bordador Juan López de Robredo, por Goya.* "Archivo Español de Arte", vol XLVII, n.º 185, 1974, pp. 81-83.

BATICLE, Jeannine: *Goya et l'Aragon du "Siècle des Lumières".* "Revue de l'Art", n.º 4-5, Paris, 1970.

— *L'activité de Goya entre 1796 et 1806 vue à travers le "Diario" de Moratín.* "Revue de l'Art", n.º 13, pp. 111-113, Paris, 1971.

— *Eugenio Lucas et les Satellites de Goya.* "Archivo Español de Arte", n.º 180, p. 428, 1972

— *Le portrait de la marquise de Santa Cruz par Goya.* "La Revue du Louvre", n.º 3, 1977, pp. 153-154.

— *Un nuevo dato sobre los Caprichos de Goya.* "Archivo Español de Arte", 1976, pp. 320-331.

— *Goya d'or et de sang.* Paris, 1986.

— *Lux ex tenebris. Goya entre la légende et la vérité.* "Colloquio" Artes 48. March 1981. Gulbenkian Foundation, Lisbon.

— and MARINAS, Cristina, with the aid of Claudine RESSORT and Chantal PERRIER: *La Galerie espagnole de Louis-Philippe*, 1838-1848. Paris, 1981.

BELTRAN, Antonio: *Goya en Zaragoza.* Premio Luzán del Excmo. Ayuntamiento. Saragossa, 1971.

BEROQUI, P.: *Una biografía de Goya escrita por su hijo.* "Archivo Español de Arte", vol. III, n.º 7, 1927.

BERUETE, A.: *Goya, composiciones y figuras.* Madrid, 1917.

— *Goya grabador.* Madrid, 1918.

— *Goya as a portrait painter.* (Transl. from the Spanish). Constable, 1922.

BOZAL, Valeriano: *Imagen de Goya.* Editorial Lumen. Barcelona, 1983.

CALVERT, A. F.: *Goya, an account of his life and works.* London, New York, 1908.

CAMON AZNAR, José: *"Los Disparates" de Goya y sus dibujos preparatorios.* Barcelona, 1951.

— *Goya en los años de la Guerra de la Independencia.* Saragossa, 1959.

— *Dibujos y grabados de Goya sobre obras de Velázquez.* "Goya", 1971.

— *Goya.* Vols. I-III, Caja de Ahorros de Zaragoza, Aragón y Rioja, Saragossa, 1980-1982.

CANELLAS see GOYA: *Diplomatario.*

CARDERERA, Valentín: *Biografía de Don Francisco de Goya.* "El Artista". Madrid, 1835.

— *Goya.* "El Semanario Pintoresco". Madrid, 1838.

CATALOGUE of the works displayed at the Ministry of Public Education and Fine Arts. Madrid, 1900.

CEAN BERMUDEZ, Juan Agustín: *Análisis del cuadro que pintó D. Francisco de Goya para la catedral de Sevilla.* 1817.

CRAWTHORNE, T.: *Goya's illness.* "Proceedings of the Royal Society of Medicine". Vol. 55, n.º 3, March 1962.

CRUZADA VILLAAMIL, G.: *Los tapices de Goya.* Madrid, 1870.

CHUECA GOITIA, Fernando: *Goya y la arquitectura.* "Revista de Ideas Estéticas". Vol. IV. n.º 15-16. Madrid, 1946.

DELTEIL, Loys: *Francisco Goya.* Vols. XIV and XV of the collection "Le Peintre Graveur Illustré". Paris, 1922.

DESPARMET FITZ-GERALD, Xavière: *L'oeuvre peinte de Goya.* Paris 1928-1950.

— *Goya. Exposition du Musée Jacquemart André.* París, 1961-62.

ENCINA, Juan de la: *Goya en Zig-Zag. Bosquejo de interpretación biográfica.* Espasa Calpe, Madrid, 1966.

EZQUERRA DEL BAYO, J.: *Iconografía de Goya.* "Arte Español", n.º 9, 1928.

— *La Duquesa de Alba y Goya.* Madrid, 1928. 2nd ed. Aguilar, Madrid, 1959.

FAUQUE, Dr. Jacques and VILLANUEVA ETCHEVERRIA, Ramón: *Goya y Burdeos. 1824-1828.* Ediciones Droel, Saragossa, 1982. (Printed in Spanish, French and English).

FLORISOONE, Michel: *En busca de Goya pintor, siguiendo a Delacroix.* "Goya", n.º 61, 1964.

— *La raison du voyage de Goya à Paris.* "Gazette des Beaux-Arts", 1175 (1966).

GALLEGO, Julián: *Las pinturas de Goya en la Cartuja de Nuestra Señora de Aula-Dei.* Saragossa, 1975.

— *Autorretratos de Goya.* Saragossa, 1978.

— *En torno a Goya.* Saragossa, 1978.

— *Goya, hombre contemporáneo* in "Conversaciones sobre Goya y el arte contemporáneo". Saragossa, 1981.

GARCIA DE PASO, Alfonso and RINCON, Wifredo: *Datos biográficos de Goya y la familia en Zaragoza.* Bulletin of the Camón Aznar Museum and Institute, Saragossa, 1981.

GARCIA DE VALDEAVELLANO, Luis: *Las relaciones de Goya con el Banco de San Carlos.* "Boletín de la Sociedad Española de Excursiones", vol. XXXVI, 1928, pp. 58-65.

GASSIER, Pierre: *Goya.* Geneva 1955.

— *Goya à Paris.* "Goya", n.º 100, 1971.

— *Une source inédite de dessins de Goya en France au XIXe siècle.* «Gazette des Beaux-Arts», May-June 1972.

— *Dibujos de Goya. Los Albumes.* 1973.

— *Vida y obra de Goya.* Juliet Wilson. Preface by Enrique Lafuente Ferrari. Ed. Juventud, Barcelona, 1974. (An English edition exists).

— *Dibujos de Goya. Estudios para grabados y*

pinturas. Ed. Noguer, Barcelona. 1975.

— *Les portraits peints par Goya pour l'infant don Luis de Bourbon à Arenas de San Pedro.* "Revue de l'Art", n.° 43, 1979, pp. 10-22.

— and WILSON, Juliet: *Goya.* Hong Kong, 1981.

GAYA NUÑO, J. A.: *La estética íntima de Goya.* "Revista de Ideas Estéticas". 1946. vol. IV.

— *La espeluznante historia de la calavera de Goya.* Rome, 1960.

— *La alegoría de la Villa de Madrid de Goya.* "Villa de Madrid", VII, n.° 27, 1969.

— *Las pinturas mitológicas de Goya.* "Goya", 1971.

GLENDINNING, Nigel: *Goya and England in the Nineteenth Century.* "The Burlington Magazine", vol. CVI, n.° 730, 1964.

— *El asno cargado de reliquias en los "Desastres de la Guerra" de Goya.* "Archivo Español de Arte", Vol. XXXV, n.° 139, pp. 221-230, 1962.

— *Goya and Arriaza's Profecía del Pirineo.* "J.W.A.C.I.", London, vol. XXVI, 1963.

— *Goya and his times at Burlington House.* "Coum" Vol. 155, n.° 623, 1964.

— *Goya's Portrait of Andrés del Peral.* "Archivo Español de Arte", n.° 165, p. 97, 1969.

— *The Strange translation of Goya's "Black Paintings".* "The Burlington Magazine", vol. CXVII, pp. 465-479, 1975.

— *Variation on the theme by Goya: Majas on a balcony.* "Apollo" vol. CIII, n.° 167, 1976.

— *Goya and his critics.* London, 1977.

— *Goya's patrons.* "Apollo". vol. CXIV, n.° 2, 1981.

— *Goya y sus críticos.* Madrid, 1982.

— *Goya's Country House in Madrid: the Quinta del Sordo.* "Apollo", 123. Feb. 1986.

GOMEZ-MORENO, Manuel: *Las crisis de Goya.* "Revista de la Biblioteca, Archivo y Museo del Ayuntamiento de Madrid". Madrid, 1935.

— *Los fondos de Goya.* Bulletin of the Academy of History commemorating the bicentenary of Goya's birth, pp. 29-41 + 17 plates, Vda. de Estanislao Maestre, Madrid, 1946.

GOMEZ DE LA SERNA, R.: *Goya.* Madrid, 1928.

GOYA, Francisco de: *Goya. Colección de cuadros y dibujos precedida de su biografía y de un epistolario.* Ed. Saturnino Calleja, Madrid, 1924.

— *Diplomatario.* Edited by Angel Canellas López.Institución Fernando el Católico, Saragossa, 1981.

— *Cartas a Martín Zapater.* Edited by Mercedes Agueda and Xavier de Salas. Ediciones Turner, Madrid, 1982.

— *Goya joven y su entorno.* Catalogue of the exhibition held in Saragossa in November-December 1986, including texts by numerous Goya experts. Camón Aznar Museum and Institute, Saragossa.

— *Goya y el espíritu de la Ilustración.* Catalogue of the exhibition held in the Prado, Madrid, Oct.-Dec. 1988, containing articles by: Alfonso E. Pérez Sánchez, Gonzalo Anes, Jeannine Baticle, Nigel Glendinning, Fred Licht and Teresa Lorenzo de Márquez.

— *Goya Nuevas Visiones. Homenaje a Enrique Lafuente Ferrari.* Edited by Isabel García de la Rasilla and Francisco Calvo Serraller. Containing articles by: Julián Marías, Francisco Calvo Serraller, Carmen Bernárdez *(Relación bibliográfica comentada de la obra del Profesor D. Enrique Lafuente Ferrari sobre Francisco de Goya),* Mercedes Agueda, Jeannine Baticle, José Luis Barrio Garay, Jan Bialostocki, Oto Bihalji-Merin, Valeriano Bozal, José Manuel Cruz Valdovinos, Fernando Chueca Goitia, Julián Gallego, Pierre Gassier, Nigel Glendinning, Edith Helman, Ilse Hempel-Lipschutz. Juan José Luna, Manuela B. Mena Marqués, John F. Moffitt, Priscilla Muller, Alfonso Emilio Pérez Sánchez, Joaquín de la Puente, Eleanor Sayre, Santiago Sebastián López, Federico Sopeña and Sarah Symmons. Amigos del Museo del Prado, Madrid, 1987.·

GUDIOL, José: *Les peintures de Goya dans la Chartreuse de l'Aula Dei à Saragosse.* "Gazette des Beaux-Arts", vol. LVII, 1105ª livraison, 1961.

— *Goya.* Milan. Garganti. 1965.

— *Goya. Biographical and Critical Study.* Thames and Hudson, London, 1966.

— *Goya, 1746-1828. Biografía, Estudio analítico y catálogo de sus pinturas.* Vol. I, text. Vols II-IV: illustrations. Ediciones Polígrafa, Barcelona, 1970.

GUERRERO LOVILLO, J.: *Goya en Andalucía,* "Goya", n.° 100, 1971.

GUINARD, Paul: *Baudelaire. Le Musée Es-*

pagnol et Goya. "Revue d'Histoire littéraire de la France", n.º 2, 1967.

— Goya et la tradition religieuse du siècle d'or. "Revue du Louvre", n.º 45, 1976.

HARRIS, Thomas: Goya: Engravings and Lithographs. Bruno Cassirer. Oxford, 1964.

HELDE, Jutta: Francisco Goya. Literatur von 1940-1962. "Z.K.", Band 28, Heft 3, 1965.

HELMAN, Edith F.: The Younger Moratín and Goya: On duendes and brujas. "Hispanic Review" vol. XXVII, n.º 1, 1959.

— Trasmundo de Goya. Madrid, 1963.

— Identity and style in Goya. "The Burlington Magazine", vol. CVI, n.º 730, 1964.

— Jovellanos y Goya. Madrid, 1970.

JUNQUERA, P.: Un lienzo inédito de Goya en el Palacio de Oriente. "Archivo Español de Arte", n.º 125-128, 1959.

KLINGENDER, F. D.: Notes on Goya's "Agony in the Garden". "The Burlington Magazine". vol. LXXXVII, n.º 48, 1940.

— Goya and the democratic tradition. London, 1948.

LAFOND, P.: Goya. Paris, 1902.

LAFUENTE FERRARI, Enrique: Los tapices de Goya en la exposición del Centenario, in "Boletín de la Sociedad Española de Excursiones". vol. XXXVI, 1928.

— Catalogue of the Goya exhibition held in the Prado, Madrid 1928.

— Goya. El dos de mayo y Los fusilamientos. Barcelona, 1946.

— Sobre el cuadro de San Francisco el Grande y las ideas estéticas de Goya. "Revista de Ideas Estéticas", n.º 15-16, vol. IV, pp. 307-337, July-December, 1946.

— La situación y la estela del arte de Goya. Essay published in the catalogue of the exhibition "Antecedentes, coincidencias e influencias del arte de Goya" held in Madrid in 1932. Sociedad Española de Amigos del Arte, Madrid, 1947.

— Goya y el arte francés. "Goya, cinco estudios", Saragossa, 1949.

— La guerra de la Independencia y Goya. "Clavileño", n.º 8, 1951.

— Los "Desastres de la Guerra" de Goya y sus dibujos preparatorios. Barcelona, 1952.

— Catalogue of the Goya exhibition, Granada, 1955.

— Goya: The frescoes in San Antonio de la Florida in Madrid, Geneva-New York, 1955.

— Boceto para la cúpula de San Antonio de la Florida. "Arte Español" vol. XXIII, 1961.

— Goya: His complete etchings, aquatints and lithographs. Thames and Hudson, London, 1962.

— Francisco Goya y Lucientes, La Tauromaquia, Club Français du livre, Paris, 1963.

— Goya, incisioni e litografía. A Vallardi, Milan, 1963.

— Goya. Collins in association with Unes, London, 1967.

— Los Caprichos de Goya. Gustavo Gili, Barcelona, 1978.

— Goya. Dibujos. Silex, Madrid, 1980.

LASSAIGNE, J.: Goya. Paris, 1948.

LEFORT, P.: Francisco Goya, étude biographique et critique, suivie d'un essai de catalogue raisonné de son oeuvre gravée et lithographiée. Paris, 1877.

LICHT, Fred: The origins of the modern temper in art. New York, 1973.

LIPSCHUTZ, Ilse Hempel: Spanish Painting and the French Romantics. Harvard University Press, Cambridge, Mass, 1972.

LOGA, V.: Goya. Berlin, 1903.

— Goya y el mundo a su alrededor. Buenos Aires, 1947.

— Francisco de Goya. Madrid, 1951.

— Goya's cast of character from the Peninsular war. "Apollo", n.º 23, 1964.

— Goya's Caprichos. Princeton University Press, 1953. Reprinted in 1970.

— Goya. Madmen and Monarchs. "Art News", New York, October 1970.

— Tradition, réalité et imagination chez Goya. "L'Oeil", n.º 292, Nov. 1979.

LOPEZ VAZQUEZ, José Manuel B.: Los Caprichos de Goya y su significado. University of Santiago de Compostela, 1982.

MALRAUX, A.: Saturne, Essai sur Goya. Paris, 1950.

MARTIN GONZALEZ, J. J.: Reflexiones sobre el arte de componer en Goya. "Goya", n.º 63, 1964.

MAYER, A. L.: Francisco de Goya. English translation by R. West, J.M. Dent, London, 1924.

— Notes on some self-portraits of Goya. "The Burlington Magazine". vol. LXIV, n.º 373. April, 1934.

MATHERON, L.: Goya. París, 1858.

MENA MARQUES, Manuela: Un nuevo dibujo

de Goya en el Museo del Prado. "Boletín del Museo del Prado", n.º 13, 1984.

MILICUA, José: *Anotaciones al Goya joven*. "Paragone", n.º 5, 1954.

MÜLLER, Priscilla E.: *Goya's Family of Charles IV*. "Apollo", n.º 96, pp. 132-137, 1970.

— *Goya's "Black Paintings", Truth and Reason in Light and Liberty*. New York, 1984.

NORDSTROM, Folko: *Goya, Saturn and Melancholy*. Stockholm, 1962.

NUNEZ DE ARENAS, Manuel: *L'Espagne des Lumières au Romantisme*. Institut d'Etudes Hispaniques, Paris, 1963.

OROZCO DIAZ, E.: *Evocación de dos obras de Goya en un Carmen de la Alhambra*. "Cuadernos de la Alhambra", n.º 2, pp. 53-58, 1966.

ORS, Eugenio D': *Goya y lo goyesco*. Madrid, 1946.

ORTEGA Y GASSET, José: *Goya*. Revista de Occidente. Col. El Arquero, Madrid, 1966.

PARDO CANALIS, E.: *La iglesia zaragozana de San Fernando y las pinturas de Goya*. "Goya", n.º 84, 1968.

— *Una visita a la galería del Príncipe de la Paz*. "Goya", n.º 148-150, 1979.

PEREZ GONZALEZ, F.: *Un cuadro de historia. Alegoría de la Villa de Madrid*. Madrid, 1910.

PEREZ SANCHEZ, Alfonso E.: *Goya: Caprichos, Desastres, Tauromaquia, Disparates*. Juan March Foundation, Madrid, 1979.

— *Goya. 120 dibujos del Museo del Prado*. Ediciones Alfiz, Madrid, 1980.

PITA ANDRADE, J. M.: *Goya ante el paisaje*. "Estudios dedicados al Profesor Emilio Orozco Díaz". University of Granada, 1979.

— *Observaciones en torno a los cartones para tapices*. "Goya", n.º 148, 1979.

— *Una miniatura de Goya*. "Boletín del Museo del Prado", n.º 1, 1980.

— *La ideología liberal en las pinturas y dibujos de Goya*. In "Goya y la Constitución de 1812", pp. 71-78 of the Catalogue of the exhibition held in the Municipal Museum, Madrid. December 1982-January 1983.

— *Goya y sus primeras visiones de la Historia*. Address on becoming a member of the Royal Academy of History. Madrid, May 21st, 1989.

PUENTE, Joaquín de la: *El retrato de Jovellanos pintado por Goya*. "B.A." n.º 34, pp. 19-20, 1974.

ROTHE, H.: *Las pinturas del Panteón de Goya, Ermita de San Antonio de la Florida*. Barcelona, 1944.

RUIZ CABRADA, A.: *Aportaciones a una bibliografía de Goya*. Madrid, 1946.

SALAS, X.: *Lista de cuadros de Goya hecha por Carderera*. "Archivo Español de Arte". vol. VII, 1931.

— *La familia de Carlos IV*. Barcelona, 1959.

— *Francisco de Goya y Lucientes*. New York, 1962.

— *Francisco José Goya*. London, 1962.

— *Retratos de artistas españolas dibujados por Goya*. "Goya", n.º 18, 1962.

— *Sobre la bibliografía de Goya (La polémica Carderera-Cruzada Villaamil)*. "Archivo Español de Arte", n.º 141, pp. 47-63, 1963.

— *Sobre un autorretrato de Goya y dos cartas inéditas sobre el pintor*. "Archivo Español de Arte". vol. XXXVII, n.º 148, pp. 317-320, 1964.

— *El Goya de Valdemoro*. "Archivo Español de Arte". vol. XXXVII, n.º 148, pp. 281-293, 1964.

— *Portraits of Spanish Artists by Goya*. "The Burlington Magazine", vol. CVI, n.º 730, 1964.

— *A group of bullfighting scenes by Goya*. "The Burlington Magazine", vol. CVI, n.º 730, 1964.

— *Sur les tableaux de Goya qui appartinrent à son fils*. "Gazette des Beaux-Arts", pág. 99, vol. LXIII, 1964.

— *Inventario de las pinturas de Don Valentín Carderera*. "Archivo Español de Arte". vol. XXXVIII, n.º 151, p. 207, 1965.

— *Los retratos de la familia Costa*. "Archivo Español de Arte". vol. XXXVII, n.º 149, pp. 64-5, 1965.

— *Francisco de Goya y Lucientes*. Barcelona, 1967.

— *Precisiones sobre pinturas de Goya: el entierro de la sardina, la serie de obras de gabinete 1793-94 y otras notas*. "Archivo Español de Arte", Madrid, 1968.

— *Fuentes de la última Comunión de San José de Calasanz*. "Goya", n.º 205, 1970.

— *Sur deux miniatures de Goya récemment retrouvées*. "Gazette des Beaux-Arts", 1973.

— *Aportaciones a la genealogía de D. Francisco de Goya*. "Boletín de la Real Academia de la Historia", vol. CLXXIV, book III, Madrid, 1977.

— *Guía de Goya en Madrid*. Madrid, 1979.
SALTILLO, Marqués del: *Miscelánea madrileña histórica y artística. Primera serie. Goya en Madrid: su familia y allegados.* (1746-1856), Madrid, 1952.
SAMBRICIO, Valentín de: *El Casticismo en los tapices de Goya.* "Revista de Ideas Estéticas", n.º 15-16, vol. IV. July-December, 1946.
— *Tapices de Goya.* Madrid, 1946.
— *Goya y la fama romántica.* "Revista de Ideas Estéticas", 1959.
SANCHEZ CANTON, Francisco Javier: *Goya en la Academia.* Real Academia de Bellas Artes de San Fernando, Madrid, 1928.
— *Los dibujos del viaje a Sanlúcar.* "Boletín de la Sociedad Española de Excursiones", vol. XXXVI, 1928, pp. 13-26.
— *Goya.* Paris, 1930.
— *La enfermedad de Goya.* "Revista Española de Arte". vol. XIII, pp. 241-8, 1934-1935.
— *Goya II. Ochenta y cuatro dibujos inéditos y no coleccionados.* Prado Museum, Madrid, 1941.
— *La elaboración de un cuadro de Goya.* "Archivo Español de Arte". vol. XVII, 1945.
— *Cómo vivía Goya.* "Archivo Español de Arte". vol. XVIII, 1946.
— *Los cuadros de Goya en la Real Academia de la Historia.* "Boletín de la Real Academia de la Historia", 1946.
— *Goya pintor religioso.* "Revista de Ideas Estéticas". vol. IV, n.º 15, 1946.
— *"Los Caprichos" de Goya y sus dibujos preparatorios.* Instituto Amatller de Arte Hispánico, Barcelona, 1949.
— *Los niños en las obras de Goya.* "Goya, cinco estudios", Saragossa, 1949.
— *The life and works of Goya.* Ed. Peninsular. Madrid, 1964.
— *Las versiones de Las Majas al balcón.* "Archivo Español de Arte". vol. XXV, 1952.
— *Los dibujos de Goya reproducidos a su tamaño y su color.* 2 vols. Prado Museum. Madrid, 1954.
— *Goya, refugiado.* "Goya, Revista de Arte", n.º 3, 1954, pp. 130-134.
— *Escultura y pintura del siglo XVIII. Francisco de Goya.* "Ars Hispaniae". Vol. XVII. Madrid, 1965.
— *Goya. La Quinta del Sordo.* Ed. Albaicin. Granada, 1966.

— and SALAS X.: *Goya and his Black Paintings.* Faber, London, 1964.
SANCHEZ RIVERO, Angel: *Los grabados de Goya.* Calleja, Madrid, 1920.
SAYRE, Eleonor A.: *Goya un momento en el tiempo.* En "Goya y la constitución de 1812", pp. 53-70 of the catalogue of the exhibition held in the Municipal Museum. Madrid, December 1982-January 1983. The same essay was published in English in the catalogue of the exhibition "Goyas Spanien. Tiden och Historien" in Stockholm.
SORIA, Martín S.: *Goya's Allegories of Fact and Fiction.* "The Burlington Magazine", July 1948, pp. 196 and ff.
TAYLOR, René: *Goya's paintings in the Santa Cueva at Cadiz.* "Apollo" vol. LXXIX, n.º 23, 1964.
TEJERO ROBLEDO, Eduardo: *El infante Luis de Borbón (1727-1785) y su estancia en Arenas de San Pedro a través de la correspondencia familiar,* "Cuadernos Abulenses", N.º 5, Jan-June 1986, pp. 215-250.
TORRECILLAS FERNANDEZ, M.ª del Carmen: *Nueva documentación fotográfica sobre las pinturas de la Quinta del Sordo.* "Boletín del Museo del Prado", n.º 17, 1985.
TRAPIER Elisabeth du Gué: *Goya, a study of his portraits 1797-99.* New York, 1955.
VIARDOT, Louis: *Etudes sur l'histoire des institutions, de la littérature, du théâtre et des Beaux-Arts en Espagne.* Paulin, Paris, 1835.
— *Notice sur les principaux peintres de l'Espagne.* Gavard, Paris, 1839.
— *Les Musées d'Espagne, d'Angleterre et de Belgique.* Paulin, Paris, 1852.
— *The School of Castille. Francisco Goya y Lucientes.* London, 1877.
VILAPLANA ZURITA, David M.: *Un grabado valenciano como fuente de "El Tres de Mayo de 1808".* Obra Social de la Caja de Ahorros de Zaragoza, Aragón y Rioja, XXIII, 1986 (containing further research into details published by Baticle in "Colloquio" in 1981).
VIÑAZA, Conde de la: *Goya, su tiempo, su vida, sus obras.* Madrid, 1887.
YRIARTE, Charles: *Goya, sa biographie, les fresques, les toiles, les tapisseries, les eaux-fortes et le catalogue de l'oeuvre.* Paris, 1867.
ZAPATER Y GOMEZ, Francisco: *Goya. Noticias biográficas.* Saragossa, 1868.

LIST OF ILLUSTRATIONS

Acknowledgments for photographs

Julio Calderón: pages 13 - 14 - 15 - 21 - 33- 41 - 45 - 49 - 65
Bank of Spain Collection: page 35
Thyssen-Bornemisza Collection: page 133
Eleonor Domínguez Ramírez: pages 22 - 23 - 27 - 31 - 39 - 43 - 47 - 51 - 52 - 53 - 55 - 61
- 63 - 67 - 71 - 75 - 78 - 79 - 81 - 83 - 84 - 87 - 93 - 97 - 101 - 103 - 105 - 107 - 108 - 109
- 111 - 112 - 113 - 115 - 117 - 119 - 121 - 123 - 125 - 127 - 131 - 135 - 137 - 139 - 141 -
142 - 143 - 145 - 147 - 149 - 151 - 153 - 155 - 157 - 159 - 161 - 165 - 167 - 168 - 169 -
175 - 177 - 179 - 181 - 183 - 185 - 187 - 188 - 189 - 190 - 191 - 192 - 197 - 198 - 199 -
201 - 203 - 204 - 205 - Front cover.
Juan Manuel Domíngez: pages 24 - 25 - 56 - 85 - 88 - 89 - 129 - 152